A MILLION MIRACLES

75 YEARS AT PHILMONT SCOUT RANCH

A MILLION MIRACLES

75 YEARS AT PHILMONT SCOUT RANCH

For Jim Mullings, my father and Scoutmaster of Troop 73.
He has lived a life of Philmont ideals.

The Donning Company Publishers
184 Business Park Drive, Suite 206
Virginia Beach, VA 23462

Steve Mull, General Manager
Barbara Buchanan, Office Manager
Heather L. Floyd, Editor
Brett Oliver, Graphic Designer
Kathy Adams, Imaging Artist
Kathy Snowden, Project Research Coordinator
Nathan Stufflebean, Marketing and Research Supervisor
Katie Gardner, Marketing Assistant

Cathleen Norman, Project Director

Library of Congress Cataloging-in-Publication Data

Mullings, David, 1958-
  A million miracles : 75 years at Philmont Scout Ranch / by David
Mullings.
      pages cm
  Includes bibliographical references.
  ISBN 978-1-57864-890-0 (hardcover : alk. paper)
1. Philmont Scout Ranch--History. 2. Camps--New Mexico--History. 3.
Boy Scouts--United States--History. I. Title.
  HS3313.Z65M65 2014
  796.54'22--dc23
                        2014000753

Printed in the United States of America at Walsworth Publishing Company

CONTENTS

PREFACE

I learned of Philmont's special charms at an early age—nine, to be exact. My parents, both school-teachers just up the road in Raton, took jobs in the summer of 1967 at the Scout Ranch's Volunteer Training Center; Dad, the center's program director, and Mom running the Small Fry, doing the daycare for the tots of the visiting families.

Philmont put our family of six up in Duplex 1A in the northern shadow of Villa Philmonte. A duplex was a tight squeeze for four kids, so we also got to use the gardener's quarters, attached to "The Big House." In Duplex 1B were the cafeteria manager, his wife, and Rusty the ornery raccoon. I'm guessing Philmont had some repair bills at 1B that winter.

For a nine-year-old, Philmont was better than Disneyland. Enrolled in the Cub Scout program, I enjoyed regular field trips to the Stockade, out under the Tooth of Time. Games, arts, buffalo barbecues, crafts, and other activities made for fun-filled days. Off-program shenanigans involved sneaking into the Big House, riding my pedal-brake bicycle with my older brother to Cimarron, and exploring the nooks and crannies of Basecamp. All summer staffers over the years get to say they had a memorable summer at Philmont; I was lucky to be able to say that years before I was a teen.

I went on to become a Boy Scout in Troop 73 of Raton, working on my Eagle. The troop couldn't muster up a Philmont contingent, so my Dad helped get me a spot on a Mountain Men trek in the summer of '74. Without enough time for an official ten-day trek, the teen boys of Training Center participants were sent out on five-day hikes. I'm a little fuzzy on the full details of our trek, a loop of the Baldy country. But I remember like it was yesterday being on the Baldy summit on the sunrise of our fourth day.

It is with that Philmont connection that I leapt at the opportunity to write a book on the seventy-fifth anniversary of Philmont Scout Ranch.

A Million Miracles: 75 Years at Philmont Scout Ranch intends to be all things to all people who have, or will soon have, a love and appreciation of this special place and thing, Philmont Scout Ranch. It intends to commemorate the rich history which preceded the founding of the Scout Ranch, and the subsequent three quarters of a century in which Boy Scouts and leaders have come to northeastern New Mexico to explore what most come to term "God's Country."

This book intends to give those who have trekked and worked at Philmont a trip down memory lane, reacquainting them with the history, the terrain, the people, and the uniqueness—all that contributed to their memorable and impacting experience.

For those new to Philmont, the book hopes to provide a comprehensive illustration of what makes Philmont tick, and how Philmont became the iconic place it is today.

A Million Miracles does not aspire to be an historical reference. Several such books have already been capably written. With goals of a reader-friendly style and broad accessibility, this tome contains no academic-style bibliography, but instead a list of sources that have been consulted in a cross-reference methodology. The author has exercised some amount of editorial license in selecting and highlighting interesting and important people and events, ones that may not have been given their historical due in past publications. Likewise, not every deserving contributor to Philmont's astounding success gains recognition here; they are simply just too numerous.

On that note, I also must add an explanation on credits for photography, or lack thereof. Cameras fire away at Philmont at a rate that likely rivals flashbulbs on the red carpet on Oscars night. Over the decades, photographs have flooded the archives at the Philmont Museum and the News and Photo Services offices, the main sources of the images featured on the following pages. That proliferation has only increased in the digital camera era. Unfortunately, not every image has been adequately labeled as to subject and photographer; in fact, the great majority of them have not, and thus many of the excellent photos deserving of publication gain only generic photo credit. I apologize to the photographers for whom credit was not possible, and am glad to report that Philmont is today engaged in an effort to organize and standardize its archival process.

After a thirty-year career in community journalism, most recently in Ouray County, Colorado, getting reacquainted with Philmont Scout Ranch, and meeting and working with the people who made it special again, for a seventy-fifth straight year, has been a labor of love.

—David Mullings

ACKNOWLEDGMENTS

In compiling material for this book, unlimited assistance and access to Philmont's archives was provided by the Philmont Museum and Seton Memorial Library, and by Philmont's News and Photo Services. My great appreciation goes out to Museum Director Dave Werhane, Librarian Robin Taylor, NPS Manager Bryan Hayek, and NPS's Patrick Breedlove, who assisted in the collection of photographs. Ed Pease, a former congressman and key Philmont and Philmont Staff Association supporter, stepped up to provide excellent last-minute editing of a raw manuscript. Finally, Cathleen Norman did a great cat-herding job of bringing the project to fruition and keeping it on track.

MOUNTAINS OF MAGIC

Special landscape, character-building programs impact lives

Philmont. It's not so much a word, a name, a place, as it is a connection, an experience, an emotional response.

At least that's the way it is to most of the million-plus outdoor-loving souls who have come to know the world's biggest and best youth adventure camp, the Philmont Scout Ranch, over the first seventy-five years of its existence.

Making Waite Phillips's big gift work in the real world requires work in three main areas. First, Philmont's core program puts crews of Boy Scout and Explorer backpackers out for eleven days onto trails that connect backcoun-

Special belt buckles commemorate the three quarters of a century that the Boy Scouts of America have made great use of their gift from Waite and Genevieve Phillips.

try camps, where the youngsters learn skills, Western lore, and about themselves. Second, the Philmont Training Center helps teach adult leaders how to best deliver the Scouting program.

Philmont's headquarters, Basecamp, occupies the eastern foot of the ridge that comes off the Tooth of Time, which has served as a geologic sentinel for Jicarilla Apache to Santa Fe Trail travelers to Boy Scouts.

And third, Philmont has remained a superbly run working cattle and buffalo ranch.

But that meat-and-potatoes rundown about what happens on these 214 square miles of beautiful New Mexican mountain country doesn't begin to relate the real story, the magic of Philmont and what the mountain experience has positively meant to so many people.

Over the years the specialness of the place has generated sayings that have become part of the Philmont lexicon. "I want to go back to Philmont!" is a constant refrain (as well as a book title, song, patch, and YouTube video) of experienced rangers and staff after their summer has ended too soon. "HOmE" has become a code acronym for Philmont: Heaven On Earth. Many a smiling ranger has proclaimed, "And they're paying me to do this!"

Many who have tasted Philmont's special sauce have attempted to describe their favorite place.

Programs and campfires at Basecamp and in the backcountry entertain—and educate—visiting Scouts.

Some of their accounts are spiritual in nature, some are life-changing, some are just fun. Here's a sampling of some of the written sentiment found in Philmont's archives:

■ Dave Caffey, on Philmont's "Who's Who" list as longtime chief ranger, and an author, wrote this in a Taos history periodical, *Ayer y Hoy en*

The first words of the last verse of the Philmont Hymn beckon Scouts to get out and find "Scouting Paradise, out in God's Country, tonight." (Photo by Matthew Prokosch, Philmont News and Photo Services)

Upon leaving a headquarters building, rangers, backcountry, and other staff are reminded of their job descriptions, and the possibilities they possess in delivering the Philmont experience.

Opposite page: A couple of coed Explorers hike a trail in the shadow of Baldy Mountain, Philmont's highest peak.

Taos, in 1988, on Philmont's fiftieth anniversary: "There is this to be said about Philmont: It is 137,000 acres of holy ground. The worst day at Philmont is to be preferred over the best day almost anywhere else. Those who have experienced Philmont tend to regard it in reverential terms—a phenomenon thought quaint by our relatives and friends. [Author] Larry Murphy called it 'a Paradise for Scouting.' The Philmont Hymn recalls a peaceful night 'out in God's Country.' Rank sentimentality? Maybe so. But it is the way we feel."

■ For sixteen years, mostly in the 1980s, Sandy Campbell Smith brought inner-city boys and girls to Philmont under the auspices of a Fort Worth Methodist church: "Joe Davis introduced me to Philmont, and my life was never the same. Philmont has inspired me, as well as countless others. Our lives have changed as a result. Philmont does change lives. It inspires and challenges the youth to depend upon others and self to become all they can be."

All Scouts and leaders leave Philmont with a lifetime's worth of memories—and the standard-issue group portrait. This one shows participants in a National Advanced Youth Leadership Experience program where older Scouts (ages fourteen to twenty) spend about a week at Rayado Ridge.

Philmont's skies never cease to amaze with their light, change, and contrasts. This sunrise lit up Cathedral Rock. (Photo by Heather Davis, Philmont News and Photo Services)

■ Jim Boeger, Rockford, Illinois Scoutmaster, led eight treks to Philmont in the 1970s and 1980s: "To me, Philmont is as close to magic as anyone can get. It is magic to watch a kid set his personal goal to meet the Philmont Challenge, tackle that challenge in spite of blisters, bears, sore feet, pinto bean suppers, and grouchy Scoutmasters, and then experience the natural high of having worked hard to meet his own goal."

■ Justin Lyon wrote for the weekly *Philnews* in 2009. In a summer-ending essay, he described nature's glories found at the ranch. Then: "Yet that only begins to describe my love for this place. Philmont has a sort of power over people. It forces growth, it breeds camaraderie. Nowhere else have I come across such a conglomerate of truly nice, interesting, and hardworking men and women.

I've never found it easier to start up conversations, to make friends, and to be accepted. Never more than now have I enjoyed waking up in the morning, earnestly looking forward to the days to come. I want to return here, and I plan to next summer. I still have so much to see and do. I want it all, the entire range of Philmont experiences."

■ John Clark has been Philmont's general manager since 2009: "During my ten-plus years here at Philmont, I have seen and heard of many stories that are meaningful, life-changing, encouraging, inspirational, and influenced by our seasonal staff. One such experience I witnessed in 2004 at Rich Cabin shows how our staff provides life-changing experiences. A crew from Detroit made up of inner-city youth arrived about mid-afternoon. After setting up camp, they came up to the cabin

A view from Urraca pairs Philmont's best-known peaks, Old Baldy and the Tooth of Time.

Backcountry staff enjoy regular views from lofty perches, such as this overlook of the Cimarroncito drainage and Webster Reservoir.

Religion remains a central tenant of Boy Scouting and at Philmont. Several outdoor chapels, including the Protestant Chapel at Base-camp, host services of many denominations.

for a tour and to do a program. One fourteen-year-old named Bobby was in awe of the livestock: pigs, chickens, cows, etc. As he was chasing a chicken, the chicken decided to take a squat and pop out an egg. Bobby went nuts! He yelled, 'I can't wait to get back home and tell Mom where eggs come from. She will never buy an egg again!' I saw Bobby a few more times during his trek and the stories he collected I am sure kept his mother in stitches for weeks after his return."

■ Carl W. Smith, crew chief, Explorer Post 16, Fort Worth: "Philmont means to me a great adventure.

It's a good way to test and show leadership qualities, test hiking and camping capabilities, and test crew togetherness. I have grown up mentally, physically, and spiritually due to Philmont. I have become a better person. Without realizing it, an important discovery was made. I learned I had control over my body... and I took control over

The Tooth of Time cradles a full moon. At the mountain's base sits the Casa de Gavilan, the stately, white-walled ranch house where Waite and Genevieve Phillips moved after donating the Villa Philmonte to the Boy Scouts of America.

my life. It's the beginning of knowing yourself, knowing you can manage yourself if you want."

■ Colleen McLaughlin Nutter, former camp director, Indian Writings, posted this on the website of the Philmont Staff Association: "Last summer I had the opportunity to spend a few hours at French

Henry, and I was instantly taken back to my backcountry days. Suddenly, the world slowed down, and I felt life in the moment. There is a beautiful thing about being off the grid, and not hearing anything but the creek, the wind, and a squeaky cabin floor. The smells of the backcountry also brought me back: pine trees, a musty cabin, and sweaty campers, which for the record, smell the same as they always did. For the first time since I worked in the backcountry, I remembered what it felt like to spend a summer working and living in the backcountry. Living was not just residing in a place, but being in the moment, embracing it, and loving every minute of it. A piece of me that I had almost forgotten was revived that day."

Powerful stuff, because Philmont's a powerful place. More than a million Scouts and Scouters have experienced Philmont's alluring attributes. Certainly, a million versions of the above testimonials could be told.

Boots, having done their work on the trail, become a collective trophy to personal achievement.

The ridges of the Sangre de Cristo Mountains captured the fancy of Waite Phillips, and perhaps a million people whose lives have been enriched by his legacy.

Moon over Urraca.

Storm over Baldy Mountain.

CHAPTER 1
PREHISTORIC TIMES

THE FIRST NATIVES

Early inhabitants hunted, gathered, and farmed in north country

Boy Scouts are but the latest *homo sapiens* to explore the wondrous land that is now northeastern New Mexico. The first human inhabitants of the Cimarron region were likely the Folsom people, who roamed the region some 10,000 years ago.

In 1908, a cowboy and former slave, George McJunkin, found a pile of bison bones that had been washed out in a flash flood near what is now the town of Folsom, about sixty miles northeast of Philmont. Further inspection led to the discovery of a distinctive fluted arrowhead lodged between two ribs of a bison. The find was historically huge. With the direct evidence of a human artifact linked to an extinct species of bison, McJunkin's discovery—which came to be known as a Folsom point—reset all assumptions of when Native Americans arrived in North America.

There exists no direct evidence that Folsom people hunted on present-day Philmont, but fragments of a Folsom point have been found on Vermejo Park, the large ranch bordering Philmont on the north.

A few thousand years later, hunting of big game as a food source declined. The people of those times, known as the Archaic Culture and lasting some

5,000 years, lived by hunting small and medium-sized game, and by gathering berries, roots, seeds, and plants. Later in the period, between 2000 and 1000 B.C., the culture delved into agriculture, growing maize.

The Anasazi Culture in the Four Corners area started roughly after 400 A.D., and this was when Native people began to occupy what is now Philmont's north country. The period was characterized by the domestic cultivation of beans, corn, and squash, and use of irrigation systems which has characterized the Pueblo Southwest.

Anasazi settlements were found along the Rio Grande and sites further east and west, such as the still-occupied pueblos of Laguna, Acoma, Zuni, and Hopi, and the long-abandoned settlements of Mesa Verde and Chaco Canyon. In the 1100s, some of the Anasazi from the Rio Grande pueblos migrated east across the Sangre de Cristo mountains to find new hunting and farming areas. They established small settlements as far east as the Vermejo River and built rock houses. These mysterious, ancient people left petroglyphs, pictures they pecked into the rock walls of North Ponil Canyon, at what is now Philmont's Indian Writings camp. By 1300, these people had abandoned their Ponil-area colonies, likely on the heels of a twenty-five-year-long drought.

A couple hundred years later, in the early 1500s, Southern Athapascans (later known as Jicarilla

A program counselor provides a history lesson about the petroglyphs found etched into the sandstone at the Indian Writings camp in the Ponil country.

Apache) began migrating from the Great Plains into the eastern foothills of the Sangre de Cristo mountains. These Indians followed herds of buffalo, depending on them for meat and skins for their tepees.

Meanwhile, further south in New Mexico, the Spanish were arriving to explore, colonize the natives, and, they hoped, find riches of gold. Coronado led an expedition through what would become mid-New Mexico in 1542, and Juan de Oñate established the first Spanish settlement in 1598, near present-day Española.

The Jicarilla Apache were known as a peaceful tribe, but with continued harassment by their old enemies from the Plains, the Utes and Comanche, the Jicarillas retreated further into Philmont's canyons. It was there the Apache met two Spanish expeditions that crossed through present-day Philmont, in 1706 (Ulibarri) and 1719 (Valverde), and established

amiable relations. The Spanish sought to subdue the marauding Comanche and protect the Jicarillas, but after the second expedition, Spanish colonization efforts and influence fizzled.

By the mid-1700s, the Jicarillas abandoned their Philmont-area settlements to seek safety from the predatory Utes and Comanche. They became more nomadic, and headed to the more populous Taos and Pecos pueblos. Gradually, tribal hostilities receded, and by the 1850s many Jicarillas were back in Cimarron country. From 1861 to 1867, they received rations from the U.S. Indian Agent in Cimarron.

In the late 1880s, the U.S. government moved the Jicarillas for good to a reservation in north central New Mexico. Today, the tribe's headquarters are in Dulce, between Taos and Farmington, and its population numbers about 3,000.

A BIG FIND

First-ever T. rex *footprint discovered at Ponil*

Long before Boy Scouts, cattle barons, frontiersmen, and Native Americans roamed the land that is now Philmont, it was likely home to one of the largest land carnivores of all time—the *Tyrannosaurus rex*.

The first-ever *T. rex* track—anywhere on the planet—was discovered in 1983 in Philmont's Ponil country by Charles Pillmore of the U.S. Geological Survey.

As no *T. rex* track had ever been identified, Pillmore was unsure what to make of his unique find. The print was first thought to possibly be that of a hadrosaur, a so-called duck-billed dinosaur, much smaller than a *T. rex*. Hadrosaur tracks have been found in the Ponil area, as well.

A full decade later, Pillmore showed a photograph of the track to Dr. Martin Lockley, a renowned British-born paleontologist working at the University of Colorado. Lockley and Pillmore traveled to the site in North Ponil Canyon in the summer of 1993, the same year Stephen Spielberg's Hollywood *T. rex* terrorized Jurassic Park on the big screen.

Lockley, noting the large size of the track—nearly three feet long, more than two feet wide, and nine inches tall—and a fourth digit, confirmed it as the first one of a *T. rex*. He published a paper of the finding the next year. The huge dinosaur, up to twenty feet tall, forty feet long, and weighing 12,000 pounds, was known as a powerful animal that could devour 500 pounds of a smaller dinosaur in one bite.

The track, and two others found at Philmont in 2009, likely date from the Late Cretaceous period of the Mesozoic Era, an estimated 66 million years ago. Paleontologist Spencer Lucas, who found

The first-ever *Tyrannosaurus rex* footprint found on the planet is fenced for historical protection.

Opposite page: Up close, Scouts study etchings from prehistoric inhabitants.

the second and third prints in 2009, called North Ponil Canyon "one of the most important sites ever found in New Mexico."

The first track has been preserved with a cage, and a to-scale track replica has been created just outside the Philmont Museum.

CHAPTER 2
CIMARRON AND THE WILD WEST

FRONTIER DAYS

Santa Fe Trail brought Wild West times to the Cimarron area

Before the 300-plus miles of trail that crisscross Philmont, there was *the* Trail: the Santa Fe Trail, the first great superhighway of trade in the American Southwest.

Over 800 long miles—the iconic route from Independence, Missouri, to its namesake city—jump-started the westward expansion of the United States and triggered a Wild West era in the Cimarron country. Previously, only fur trappers and traders, and some Spanish explorers, had wandered into the Rocky Mountains in search of beaver. Among those mountain men who trekked through what would become northern New Mexico were Kit Carson, Lucien Maxwell, and William and Charles Bent, all of who would play major roles in the region's history.

The Santa Fe Trail was first traveled in 1821, the same year that Mexico gained independence from Spain. Both events would impact the land around Cimarron. The trail had two branches: one direct from the plains of Kansas southwest to Santa Fe (called the Cimarron Cutoff, because it did just that at Cimarron, Kansas), and the second, the Mountain Branch that headed west to Bent's Fort and then the mountains, over Raton Pass, and

Lucien B. Maxwell managed his father-in-law's immense landholdings from Rayado for nearly a decade. In 1857, he established the town of Cimarron and began to acquire the Beaubien-Miranda land grant acreage. (Courtesy of the Philmont Museum archives)

through Cimarron, New Mexico. Though longer, the Mountain Branch was considered safer from Indian attacks with better water availability and scenically refreshing after the long slog across the boring plains. Philmont's Tooth of Time mountain rock face was perhaps the most striking of many landmarks along the route.

Caravans of wagon trains carted goods and supplies to Santa Fe to be distributed in the Mexican

Maxwell's house, illustrated in this painting, was a lively hub of activity along the Cimarron River, near his three-story gristmill. (Courtesy of the Philmont Museum archives)

markets, which, unlike the Spanish, welcomed the American trade. The Santa Fe Trail would continue to be well traveled until about 1880, when the Atchison, Topeka & Santa Fe Railroad forged into New Mexico on a route nearly identical to the old trail, and with much track built right over the old wheel ruts.

Twenty years after the advent of the Santa Fe Trail, a second significant event would impact development in the Cimarron area—creation of the Land Grant. In 1841, two Mexican citizens, Charles Beaubien and Guadalupe Miranda (Beaubien was born in Canada, but married a Mexican woman and became a Mexican citizen), were granted a huge rectangle of land that stretched at its northern edge from the Spanish Peaks east to what is now Trinidad, Colorado, and at the south border in New Mexico from Angel Fire to Springer. Beaubien and Miranda were charged with settling the acreage, but soon an American flag would fly over the lands as a result of the Mexican-American War.

The fur trapper Lucien B. Maxwell, an Illinois native, had settled in Taos in 1841, and married Beaubien's daughter Luz in 1844. With the Mexican

war settled in 1848, Maxwell led settlers east out of Taos to Rayado, at the south-central edge of the Beaubien-Miranda grant, a strategic site for routes to Santa Fe and Taos. A year later, Kit Carson, likely weary of his participation in the war and Indian fighting campaigns, agreed to partner with Maxwell and settle at Rayado.

Maxwell's colony prospered with pastures for cattle, sheep, and horses. Hay and other crops were raised. But in the first years, raiding Indians posed a threat to the new community. A company of U.S. Dragoons was sent to Rayado in 1850 to protect the colony and continuing traffic on the Santa Fe Trail from Indians. In 1851, Fort Union was established thirty miles down the trail, bringing added security to Rayado.

One story has been passed down as part of Rayado's lore. About 600 marauding Apache surrounded the fort at Rayado, with about sixty people inside. With

After Maxwell sold his land, the foreign investors had grand designs to make their investment reap profits, as this promotional brochure shows. (Courtesy of the Philmont Museum archives)

Lucien Maxwell made his fortune from agriculture, real estate sales, and mining. The Aztec strike triggered the gold rush on Baldy. Here, mining families inhabit the Jackson Boarding House at Baldy Town. (Courtesy of the Philmont Museum archives)

Kit Carson's attempt to settle down to life as a farmer at Rayado was short-lived. (Courtesy of the Philmont Museum archives)

precious little time before the Indians would attack over the fort walls, Vidal Trujillo, a son-in-law of Charles Beaubien, volunteered to ride to Fort Union, thirty miles to the south. He saddled up the finest thoroughbred, Rayado, and the fort gate was thrown open. The big chestnut horse shot into the midst of the circling raiders. Crouched low, Vidal, an accomplished horse racer, guided him through the surprised Indians. They gave pursuit, but Trujillo and Rayado made the escape, and he pushed the horse hard to Fort Union. Upon arrival, the exhausted Rayado fell beneath Trujillo, ridden to a heroic death. The Indians, knowing that military help was imminent, had given up their attack.

Kit Carson's stay at Rayado was not long. He was appointed Indian agent at Taos in 1854, allowing his wife Josefa to be reunited with her prominent Taos family.

After nine years at Rayado, Lucien Maxwell moved north eleven miles and created a new ranch on the Cimarron River. It thrived and became the town of Cimarron, with hundreds of workers running livestock and farming irrigated fields. Maxwell ruled his lands as a benevolent dictator, wielding full control over the laborers, but treating them fairly. Maxwell built a three-story gristmill to grind wheat

from his fields. The Old Mill stands alongside the Cimarron River today, a museum of the region's rich history.

In 1858, Maxwell bought out Guadalupe Miranda's half-share of the granted land, making him a partner with his father-in-law. The price: $2,745. When Charles Beaubien died in 1864, Maxwell and his wife Luz inherited more of the grant, and soon they bought the rest of the claims from other Beaubien heirs. The newly named Maxwell Land Grant encompassed 1,714,764 acres, or about 2,700 square miles. The largest land grant in United States history, it is just slightly less than the combined acreage of fourteen ranches—about 2 million acres—accumulated in recent times by media mogul Ted Turner.

Maxwell's big acquisition coincided with a gold rush. The precious metal was found on and around Mount Baldy in 1866, and over the hill at Elizabethtown. Miners flooded into the area in search of ore. The already-wealthy Maxwell grew richer from gold strikes. He was a partner in the most productive mine in the district, the Aztec, and collected gold and payments from squatting miners working on his land.

The Stone Face, etched anonymously into a sandstone outcropping west of Cimarron, is cloaked in mystery. Some say it is a likeness of outlaw Black Jack Ketchum, a lookout over the plains. (Courtesy of the Philmont Museum archives)

But as with a later owner of Cimarron-area acreage, Waite Phillips, there was more to life for Maxwell than just money. The rush of tens of thousands of people into the mining camps changed things forever. Maxwell, the largest landowner in the United States, was quoted as saying that he "was tired of this place, from the Indians and the new-comers on the land." He and Luz decided to sell and move.

A transaction came together quickly in 1870. A group headed by a Colorado senator and members of the notorious Santa Fe Ring acquired the grant

for a sum of about $650,000 and then sold it three months later, at double the profit, to an English syndicate. Soon, tensions began rising as the new landowners began cracking down on Land Grant settlers who Maxwell had treated casually. In five years, the tensions would boil over into the Colfax County War.

After the sale of his land grant, Lucien Maxwell would live just five more years. He and Luz moved south to Fort Sumner, which had just been de-militarized. Maxwell's interests in banking and a railroad were failures, and when he died in 1875 from pneumonia, his riches had dwindled to nothing. A footnote to the Maxwell story occurred six years later. Sheriff Pat Garrett shot William "Billy the Kid" Bonney dead in a bedroom of the Maxwell house, and the outlaw, who was a friend of Maxwell's son Pete, came to be buried very near Lucien Maxwell. At least that's the most common version of this Wild West lore. Another folk tale, which continued to be investigated well into the twenty-first century, was that Garrett shot another man who was set up by Bonney, and the outlaw then fled to Texas and lived out his days under an alias.

FIFTEEN YEARS OF CONFLICT

Colfax County War centered on land grant use, disputes

Nearly a century and a half ago, the parcels that became Philmont were center stage in a bloody conflict over control of that land.

In May 1887, the U.S. Supreme Court ruled to confirm the validity of the Maxwell Land Grant. The decision effectively ended the infamous Colfax County War, fifteen years of conflict, violence, and killings in and around Cimarron, the center of the Rhode Island-sized piece of prized land holdings.

Tensions first arose after Lucien Maxwell sold his massive land holdings in 1870. The British inves-

The Rev. O. P. McMains, seeking to avenge the killing of a fellow pastor, Rev. Franklin Tolby, made the declaration of war on the British landowners and their Santa Fe politician allies. (Courtesy of the Philmont Museum archives)

tors who purchased the 1.7 million acres expected, of course, to profit from their land. When Maxwell, somewhat of a benevolent dictator, left town, so did his practice of "getting along" with the itinerant ranchers, farmers, miners, and squatters who worked the vast Land Grant acreage. Now, the British-held Maxwell Land Grant Company treated these people as unwelcome squatters and demanded compensation.

Issues of money and religion commonly exist at the start of armed conflicts. The Colfax County War involved elements of both.

As friction grew from heavy-handed policies of the new Land Grant owners, a Methodist minister, the Rev. Franklin Tolby, sided with the settlers and became a vocal critic. On September 14, 1875, he was found shot to death in Cimarron Canyon. His untouched belongings indicated that robbery was not a motive. If the killing was meant to intimidate the people working the land into silence, it did exactly the opposite. The war had begun.

A second minister and friend of Rev. Tolby, the Rev. O. P. McMains, took up the crusade against the British company and its allies of powerful New Mexico politicians, known as the Santa Fe Ring. Rev. McMains declared: "The war is on; the precious blood of settlers has been shed, and we must fight it out on this line. No quarter now for the foreign land thieves and their hired assassins."

A central issue in the conflict was the permissible size of a land grant, and even Maxwell, before his sale, had ignored a territorial ruling that a single grant could not exceed an area of twenty-two leagues (about 168,000 acres), a bit larger than present-day Philmont. The Beaubien-Miranda and Maxwell land size had grown to more than ten times greater, 1,714,764 acres.

This bad blood resulted in a decade-plus of spilled blood. As many as 200 people were killed in the conflict as raids, arson, violence, cattle rustling, lawlessness, and vigilante justice prevailed in the Cimarron area. The resisting settlers came to call themselves the Colfax County Ring, and gunslinger Clay Allison became the most notorious of those fighting the establishment forces. Allison led the lynching of a Santa Fe-supported constable, Cruz Vega, who was suspected by the mob of involvement in Rev. Tolby's death. Allison and his brother chased a Santa Fe Ring-appointed probate judge, Dr. Robert Longwell, to Fort Union, but failed to catch him before he reached the safety of the fort's walls.

At one point, the influential grant owners persuaded the New Mexico territorial governor, Lionel Sheldon, to assemble a military force, and thirty-five troops were gathered in Trinidad, Colorado, just north of the Land Grant boundary. But across Raton Pass, a posse of ranchers organized and bought up all available guns and ammunition. The outgunned militia was marched back to Colorado.

The legal issues chugged through the court systems, and finally, the U.S. Supreme Court's 1887 decision brought certainty to the situation. The Maxwell Land Grant Company—at the time owned by a group from the Netherlands after the English firm went into foreclosure in 1879—could definitively sell and lease its lands or drive out the settlers. The company's control was complete.

A few last gasps at establishing homesteaders' claim likewise failed. In 1888, several people were killed as violence erupted at the far northwest reaches of the grant, in Stonewall, Colorado. A final legal challenge ended in 1894 with another Supreme Court ruling wholly rejecting homesteader assertions.

The final nail in the coffin of the Maxwell-era quasi-public use of the land came in 1902, when wealthy Chicago grain baron William Barlett bought 205,000 acres along the Vermejo River. Barlett conditioned his purchase of what is now Vermejo Park that the sellers "are given two years to get the Mexicans off."

LOCOMOTIVES INTO CIMARRON

Railroads played brief role in the region's development

The first rails came in 1906 to service the mining boom in the Baldy Mountain area and a coal mine, Koehler, between Raton and Cimarron. The St. Louis, Rocky Mountain & Pacific Railroad laid ninety-five miles of track from Des Moines, New Mexico, through Cimarron and terminating at Ute Park.

The Continental Tie & Lumber Co. owned the Cimarron & Northwest Railway Co., created to haul its timber out of Ponil. (Courtesy of the Philmont Museum archives)

Charles Springer was instrumental in luring Harry Koehler to invest in Colfax County. Koehler, president of the American Brewing Company in St. Louis, went on to become chairman of the board of directors of the Maxwell Land Grant Company.

In addition to the main Des Moines-Ute Park line, the St. Louis Rocky Mountain had a six-mile spur from the Clifton House on the Santa Fe Trail to Raton and a short section from Koehler Junction to the coal mine company town of Koehler, near what is now known as Hoxie Junction. Within a year after the rails arrived, Koehler boasted a thriving population of about 1,000, eventually growing to 1,800.

The St. Louis Rocky Mountain operated for just thirteen years, as railroads started converting from coal to diesel fuel around 1920. With the decrease in coal demand, towns, mines, and railroads were abandoned.

The second rail line, the Cimarron & Northwest Railway Co., ran exclusively in what is now Philmont's north country, Ponil, to provide transport for timber operations. The rail was created by Thomas Schomburg as a subsidiary of his Continental Tie & Lumber Co., and financial backing for the C&N was provided by William Barlett, the Chicago grain dealer who bought the Vermejo Park ranch north of Philmont. Construction started in 1907, and the railway's first section traversed twenty-two miles from Cimarron to Ponil Park, with a later stretch covering thirteen miles into Bonito Park.

The rails climbed 1,400 feet in elevation and chugged over fifty-one bridges. The company's stock consisted of five boxcars (mainly for mining equipment and ore transport), thirty-nine flat cars (for timber), one caboose, and Engine No. 1, known as "Sallie." The value of the rail stock was pegged at $20,693.

Similar to the St. Louis Rocky Mountain, the C&N's life was short-lived. With timber supplies

A C&N train rolls into the Continental sawmill at Bonito. (Courtesy of the Philmont Museum archives)

Continental Tie & Lumber workers pause for a pose at the sawmill. (Courtesy of the Philmont Museum archives)

depleted, sections were abandoned in 1916 and 1923. All operations ceased in 1930.

The C&N had early designs on expanding westward, and surveyed a route into the Moreno Valley and on to Taos. But the daunting task of getting over McAvoy Hill and into Eagle Nest was never solved.

After seventy-five years, Philmont's railroad legacy is getting its due. Under a project begun in 2013, Philmont will have a staffed backcountry interpretive camp dedicated to telling the region's rail history and giving Scouts hands-on experience at a working rail depot.

On the old C&N line into Ponil, a telephone station about halfway in was known as the Metcalf Station, named for William Metcalf, a Colfax County sheriff's deputy who was ambushed and killed during the 1870s war. Over the years Philmont has known this site as Old Camp.

Plans for the new Metcalf Station camp call for two and a half miles of track to be built on the old railbed. Scouts will be able to travel the section on hand, or pump, rail cars. They will learn about the communication methods of the early 1900s with a usable telegraph line. Crews may be able to camp in old cattle and rail cars, too.

DIVIDING THE GRANT

Ambitious ranchers carved spreads out of Maxwell lands

The late 1800s and early 1900s were a time of transition on the land that was to become Philmont. After the Colfax County War and before Waite Phillips bought ranch land some twenty-five years later, the acreage that made up the Maxwell Land Grant was chopped up and divvied, piece by piece, into numerous ranches. Coinciding with these changes to the Cimarron region landscape were booms and busts in two significant industries in early Colfax County—railroads and mining.

The saga of the ranching spreads during this era includes its share of characters, tragedies, and events that molded Philmont as we know it today.

Take the Urraca Ranch, for instance. What is most readily identified as Philmont today, the Basecamp headquarters and the Tooth of Time area, developed from the Urraca operation, one of the first acreages to be split off the Maxwell Land Grant. Lucien Maxwell and his father-in-law, Charles Beaubien, sold the Urraca parcel in 1861 to Peter Joseph, who, like Kit Carson, appeared to be ready to settle down and farm in the Rayado area after years of mountain man life. Joseph, however, died a year later. Little is known about Joseph's young son who inherited the property, which was little used until 1880 when it was acquired by a back-east stock market player named Frank Sherman.

Sherman had bought large blocks of stock and bonds in the Maxwell Land Grant Company, and after buying the Joseph holding, added to the acreage under his control by leasing a good chunk of company land to the north. However, horses, not cattle, were Sherman's interest. The locals took note as a number of English thoroughbreds arrived at the train station in nearby Springer. Sherman developed his property as a fine horse farm, which was

likely the genesis of a long tradition of high-quality thoroughbreds and quarter horses being raised and raced in Colfax County, including the La Mesa Park track that operated in Raton for nearly fifty years. But Sherman's time on the New Mexico ranch wasn't long. After just five years, in 1885, Sherman sold to the English-born Francis Clutton, who had been ranching with much difficulty on the eastern plains of Colfax County. The Urraca spread, nestled up to the Sangre de Cristo mountains, lured Clutton to the ideal location as it did ranchers and speculators before and after him.

Clutton's tenure would be both productive, and eventually, tragic. He quickly put the land back in cattle production, irrigated pastures to produce alfalfa as winter feed, and married the daughter of the manager of the Maxwell Land Grant Company. Clutton thrived, then introduced a new means to profit in the cattle business—selling off calves to be shipped to the big cities back east. All was good as long as the cattle market was good. But markets go up, and they go down. Clutton was soon caught up in a major reversal of fortune. He borrowed $30,000, but with the downturn in the cattle industry, couldn't make his first payment, due in 1894. Clutton ended up working a lease of his entire 80,000 acres to William French, a Civil War veteran who owned a spread near Socorro, and came to own a second between Springer and Cimarron, known to this day as the French Tract.

Clutton's ranching days were over; he lost all his New Mexico holdings to foreclosure and tax sales and moved his family to Denver. The last five years of the nineteenth century provided no improvement to Clutton's hard times. One day in November 1901, Clutton went to a bar, had a beer and a cigar, and then shot himself in the forehead.

The Clutton ranch was leased, then sold, to Stanley McCormack, the son of Cyrus McCormack, the Chicago inventor and manufacturer of the grain reaper. McCormack's

Cowboys of the Maxwell Cattle Co. prepare for a chuckwagon feast during a roundup. (Courtesy of the Philmont Museum archives)

emergence on the scene was a notable precursor in two areas. He was next in line as a monied gentleman rancher around Cimarron, interested in the recreational possibilities in addition to the mere ranching potential. He also landed there partially because of health reasons, a respiratory ailment. But it was a mental health issue, dementia, that soon incapacitated McCormack, and caused his wife to dispose of his 70,000 acres in 1910. The land was turned over to the ranch manager, George Webster Jr., at a price of $125,000. The McCormacks moved to an estate near Santa Barbara, California, where McCormack remained in an impaired state until his death in 1947. The McCormack saga inspired a 1998 novel, *Riven Rock*, the name of their California estate.

The ambitious Webster, the last Urraca Ranch owner until Waite Phillips, would have a huge impact on what would become Philmont. Webster embarked on numerous irrigation projects, built

reservoirs, planted large apple orchards that would bear prize-winning fruit, constantly worked to improve his cattle stock, built a fishing lodge, stocked his lakes, had his ranch declared a state game preserve, and, notably, invited some Boy Scouts to visit and explore in the summers of 1916 and 1917.

Webster's good, early success at the Urraca Ranch began to fade with a down cycle in the cattle business and tightening of credit. He put 44,000 acres up for sale in 1922. The buyer was one Waite Phillips. Webster sold the Tulsa oilman his remaining 30,000 acres the following year.

Among other prominent Cimarron-area ranchers in those years were: the Abreu family of the Rayado area; M. M. Chase, with a spread in the Ponil country, a ranch that was in the family up until 2013 when Philmont was given its lease (more on this elsewhere); H. M. Porter, who came to own about 25,000 acres of pastureland east of the Clutton and Abreu places; and two smaller operations, run

Fred Lambert, son of St. James Hotel proprietor Henri Lambert, served as an important sheriff and lawman through the early 1900s. He went on to become a local historian and friend of Philmont into the 1960s. (Courtesy of the Philmont Museum archives)

by Mathias Heck and J. M. Nash respectively. The ranches, part or all of which would become the property of Waite Phillips in the 1920s, each have their own rich histories to tell.

No telling of Cimarron ranching would be complete, however, without an accounting of the Springer brothers, Frank and Charles.

Frank Springer moved from his native Iowa to Cimarron in 1873, just as tensions were rising in what would be the Colfax County War. Over his next ten years in Cimarron, Springer, as legal counsel to the Maxwell Land Grant Company, played a huge role in how the region would be developed. He litigated and won the Supreme Court case that validated the grant and the company's control. He also served as president of the Land Grant firm and led the development of its resources.

After Cimarron, Frank Springer pursued civic projects further south in New Mexico, helping form New Mexico Highlands University in Las Vegas and the Museum of New Mexico in Santa Fe. Springer avidly studied paleontology, and collected

a unique type of fossil. The collection was donated to the Smithsonian Institution.

Charles Springer, ten years Frank's junior, followed his older brother to New Mexico in 1878. He concentrated on the cattle business with great success. He married a daughter of rancher M. M. Chase, and bought a sizable tract from the rancher. The large CS Ranch, Philmont's longtime neighbor, remains headquartered just outside Cimarron and continues to be run by family descendants of Charles Springer.

Notably, the brothers were granted a permit in 1907 from Territory of New Mexico officials to dam the Cimarron River at its exit from the Moreno Valley. The Eagle Nest Dam began construction eleven years later. The CS Ranch operated the dam and lake until 2002, when it was sold to the State of New Mexico. It is the largest privately constructed dam in the United States. Philmont owns 1,000 acre-feet of junior water rights in the lake.

CHAPTER 3
THE WAITE PHILLIPS STORY

WAITE PHILLIPS

*Restless entrepreneur, philanthropist
lived classic American life*

Befitting a wealthy oilman, Waite Phillips employed a chauffeur. But Waite Phillips wasn't one to easily cede control of a situation, so he was often at the wheel of his motorcar while his hired driver rode in the back seat.

That was the case in 1941, according to one account, when Phillips met in a car with Walter Head, president of the Boy Scouts of America. Three years earlier, Phillips had gifted about 36,000 acres of the north part of his ranch and $61,000 in operating funds, and the Boy Scouts had it up and running as the Philturn Rockymountain Scoutcamp. He and the Scouting executive were out to inspect the camp in the Ponil canyons.

According to Ralph "Woodie" Erwin, Phillips' executive secretary at the time (as retold by son Bill Erwin, who heard the story many times), Phillips and Head were in the front seats, Erwin and the chauffeur, Maurice Shrewsbury, in the back. Phillips made his verbal offer of the second gift to the BSA—a bigger chunk of Philmont ranch, including Villa Philmonte, the stately summer mansion of the Phillips family. The BSA president expressed reservations and threw up objections, explaining that the organization would be over-

Waite Phillips signed this portrait to the Boy Scouts to be displayed at the Villa Philmonte. (Courtesy of the Philmont Museum archives)

whelmed to manage such a large tract of land and its vast resources.

Waite Phillips was undeterred, and likely had anticipated the reluctance of the Scout leaders. He added to the offer his twenty-three-story Philtower Building in Tulsa and a portfolio of municipal bonds, adding lucrative income sources to support the Philmont program and operation. "My

In the truest sense of the word, Waite, left, and Wiate were identical twins, and inseparable. (Courtesy of the Philmont Museum archives)

dad said it was the strangest negotiation he ever encountered," recalled Bill Erwin, who grew up at Philmont and went on to become an attorney in nearby Raton. "Especially considering the toughness with which Mr. Phillips usually negotiated."

In the same month that the Japanese attacked Pearl Harbor and the United States entered World War II, Head took the offer to the National Executive Board. The Boy Scout bosses, recognizing the immense possibilities of an expanded camping program, could not say no.

On the final day of 1941, 91,538 acres of central and south Philmont were transferred from Waite and Genevieve Phillips to the Boy Scouts of America. The Philturn Rockymountain Scoutcamp grew to become Philmont Scout Ranch, all thanks to a benevolent and insistent Oklahoma oilman.

The story of Waite Phillips has been well chronicled. It is a classic tale of American success.

Waite was born in January 1883 into a large family in Conway, Iowa, minutes after an identical twin, Wiate. The twins grew up in rural Iowa and left home at age sixteen, bitten by the bug of wanderlust and tales of the Wild West. Their dreams extended far beyond Iowa and the family farm. Waite and Wiate meandered for nearly three years mainly through the northern Rocky Mountains, enjoying adventures such as hopping freight trains, trap-

The entire Phillips family, Waite, Helen Jane, Chope, and Genevieve, took to the Western way of life. (Courtesy of the Philmont Museum archives)

Waite Phillips first christened his newly bought spread outside Cimarron as the Hawkeye Ranch, in honor of his native Iowa. (Courtesy of the Philmont Museum archives)

ping in the Bitterroot Mountains, and working as Western Union delivery boys in Salt Lake City. One imagines that the challenges of nomadic life away from family, and on the American frontier, made for a character-building experience for the twins, perhaps portending a future donation whose main aim was to facilitate maturity and character in teenaged boys. The Phillips twins were coming of age.

Phillips soon changed the name of his ranch to Philmont, a combination of his name and the Spanish word for mountain. (Courtesy of the Philmont Museum archives)

But tragedy struck in 1902, when Wiate suffered a burst appendix. He died in a Catholic hospital in Spokane, Washington.

Waite was devastatingly distraught—the twins were identical in every way and inseparable. Still, the teenaged adventures had instilled in him a love of the mountains and ranchlands. He returned to Iowa, and enrolled in a business college. He graduated, became a bookkeeper at a coal company and

then a salesman, and met and married a banker's daughter, Genevieve Elliot, in 1909.

Over the next twenty years, Phillips enjoyed a fast and prosperous rise in the business world. He followed two older brothers, Frank and L. E., to Oklahoma, where they invested in the burgeoning oil business. Phillips started on the ground floor of the exploration and production industry as a roustabout, and worked as his brothers' man in the field until 1914. The older Phillips brothers divested most of their oil holdings, choosing to concentrate on banking. The hiatus would last three years before the Phillips Petroleum Company was established by Frank and L. E. and went on to become a huge multinational corporation, Phillips 66.

The younger Phillips, though, moved to Fayetteville, Arkansas, and started a wholesale gasoline and service station distributorship. The business proved to be too slow-paced for him. In 1916, Phillips moved back to Oklahoma and

Phillips's favorite place at Philmont was the Rayado Lodge, now known as Fish Camp. (Courtesy of the Philmont Museum archives)

Genevieve Phillips, by all accounts, was a loving soulmate for her husband. Here, she is pictured at the pool of the Villa Philmonte. (Courtesy of the Philmont Museum archives)

bought an oil lease in Okmulgee. He made his first significant fortune by selling the successful lease to the Atlantic Petroleum Company.

From there, it was off to the financial races. Waite and Genevieve moved to Tulsa in 1918, and he organized the Waite Phillips Company in 1922. In three years' time, the firm was producing about 40,000 barrels of oil a day and was worth tens of millions. In 1925, at age forty-three, Phillips sold out to a Wall Street investment firm for $24.8 million in cash. The company's workers shared $2 million in purchased stock and bonuses. Phillips also used $800,000 in 1925 to prop up his father-in-law's ailing bank in Knoxville, Iowa.

On the personal side of life, Waite and Genevieve started a family. Helen Jane was born in 1911, and Elliot came along in 1918. And Phillips had made his first foray into Rocky Mountain real estate, purchasing a ranch near Denver that he called "Highland," eventually developed by other investors into the Highlands Ranch suburban development.

The mostly flat Colorado property never fit Phillips's fancy, and in 1922, he sent his Denver ranch manager to Cimarron, New Mexico, to check out the Urraca Ranch, for sale southwest of town. After a favorable report, Phillips bought about 42,000 acres for $150,000. The next year, he added 30,000 more acres. Contiguous properties, including mountain acreage still held by the Maxwell

Land Grant Company, became available, and Phillips scooped them up. By 1926, Philmont (the ranch's second name; the first was Hawkeye, for his native Iowa) had grown to almost 300,000 acres. In 1927, the twenty-two-room Mediterranean-inspired Villa Philmonte mansion was completed, becoming the summer home of the Phillips family for the next fifteen years, a cool retreat from sweltering Tulsa summers.

Instead of retiring to Philmont after the multi-million dollar sale of his namesake company, Waite Phillips dived right back into the oil business. He organized another business, Philmack Oil, and acquired controlling interest in another, Independent Oil & Gas, and merged the two. In the following years, Independent would grow to assets of about $68 million, with refineries in Okmulgee and Kansas City.

But hard times were ahead. The Great Depression hit, and fortunes at the older Phillips brothers' company plummeted. In 1930, Phillips 66 and Independent merged to create a stronger company to survive the Depression. Waite Phillips never became actively involved in the management of the enlarged company. Son Elliot "Chope" Phillips later told historians that Waite and Frank, the visionary of the two older brothers, were both just too headstrong. In fact, they had earlier competed with each other for oil leases, but had also partnered up on occasion. Despite mutual respect and admiration, Chope recalled, "they just couldn't get along. The reason is that if two men are riding on the same trail, one has to be in front."

With his usual foresight and good timing, Waite Phillips survived the onset of the Great Depression relatively unscathed. He had much of his fortune invested in municipal bonds, as opposed to the decimated stock market. Phillips, however, had earlier taken a large interest in the First National Bank of Tulsa, and had served as its chairman since 1927. At considerable cost, he ended up personally liquidating millions of dollars of underwater real estate loans, where their values were worth far less what was owed.

Through the 1930s, and out of the oil business—though there were lingering complications after he ceded control of the merged company to his brothers—Phillips was occupied with helping friends and family deal with Depression-caused financial complications, managing his Oklahoma and New Mexico properties, dealing with family matters (daughter Helen Jane gave birth to a second child, then suffered through a divorce, and Chope's young life was at a crossroads), and increasingly, spending time in Southern California. Under Phillips's methodical and demanding guidance, Philmont had been developed into one of the best ranch operations in the American West. It employed as many as fifty ranch hands and ran up to 3,000 head of cattle and 9,000 sheep.

But for some time, Phillips had had higher purposes in mind for his prized property. He had contacted the Boy Scouts of America as early as 1930 to explore the options of using his acreage to benefit boys. He renewed a contact in 1937, and, in 1938, donated the Ponil country that became Philturn Rockymountain Scoutcamp. That same year, a month earlier, Waite and Genevieve donated their Tulsa home estate, Philbrook, to the City of Tulsa to be home of an art museum. They moved into a downtown apartment and spent considerable time at Philmont.

Then, in 1941, he conducted the second round of negotiations with the Boy Scouts, and Philturn ballooned into Philmont, growing from 36,000 to 127,000 acres. In both donations, Phillips stipulated that he would retain no control on how the Boy Scouts operated their new property. But that didn't prevent him from keeping tabs on their progress, or offering sometimes pointed observations on their operations.

True to Phillips's restless nature and his saying that the only permanent thing is change, Waite

Waite Phillips, at the auto court entrance to the Villa. (Courtesy of the Philmont Museum archives)

and Genevieve left Tulsa in 1945 for Los Angeles. Phillips would live out his years there, still busy in real estate transactions, staying in contact with the Boy Scouts, and continuing his philanthropic work, including at the University of Southern California. He suffered the first of what would be many heart attacks through the rest of his life in December 1947.

Though Waite Phillips had given up residence in New Mexico, it was clear from his voluminous correspondence with Boy Scout executives over the next two-plus decades that his thoughts were never far from Philmont. His last visit to Philmont was in 1955, but as late as a month before his death, he dispatched his son Chope to check on affairs at the ranch and file a written report to him. After a series of heart attacks, Waite Phillips died in Los Angeles at age eighty-one on January 27, 1964.

Services were held at the Westwood Memorial Park Cemetery, where Marilyn Monroe had been laid to rest two years earlier.

In a 1948 interview, Waite Phillips laid out his rationale for his Philmont donation. "During all the years I worked in developing this property and in trying to restore the land to usefulness by conservation methods, I received much physical, mental, and spiritual values from it. Our young son, who spent much of his boyhood and adolescent years on it during vacations, received similar benefits. Therefore it seemed natural that it be donated for the benefit of millions of young Americans with the hope they might receive equal benefits."

THE BIG HOUSE

Villa Philmonte, constructed in tandem with the Phillips family Tulsa home

To some, it may seem a bit odd that the world's preeminent high-adventure camp for youth might include a unique Spanish-style mansion at its headquarters. Philmont Scout Ranch proudly features just such a structure: the magnificent Villa Philmonte.

When Waite and Genevieve Phillips made their second, larger gift in 1941, it included almost all of the ranch properties the family had assembled starting about two decades previous. Among those transferred assets were mountain outposts such as the Rayado Lodge (Fish Camp) and Cimarroncito, all the ranching infrastructure and buildings, and, of course, the Villa Philmonte.

The opulent residence adds an interesting, if unlikely, dimension to the unparalleled Philmont experience.

Once Waite Phillips made big money in big oil, he was not reluctant to spend it. In 1925, after the multi-million-dollar sale of his self-named oil company, he began planning for the simultaneous construction of not one, but two mansions for the Phillips family. One would become Villa Philbrook, the family's main home about two miles south of downtown Tulsa. The second, the Villa Philmonte, would be the Phillipses' cool summer retreat on their scenic New Mexico ranch.

Afternoon light bathes the Villa Philmonte and its grounds, as seen in 2012.

The Villa from the courtyard. (Photo by Rachel Taylor, Philmont News and Photo Services)

The Big House's front lawn catches shadows. (Photo by Matthew Prokosch, Philmont News and Photo Services)

In the oil business, Waite Phillips was notorious for his meticulous planning, hard work, attention to detail, and standards of excellence. He was no different when it came to the building of his two mansions; happenstance was not an option. The first order of home-building business involved the selection of an architect. Through business, Phillips had befriended one J. C. Nichols, of Kansas City. In the early 1920s, Nichols had conceived of and built the Country Club Plaza, the first-ever suburban shopping center, designed to cater to newly mobile customers arriving in automobiles. Nichols settled on a Spanish Colonial Revival style for his groundbreaking development, and selected as his architect Edward Buehler "Ned" Delk, a Pennsylvania native who had spent considerable time studying in Europe. After Country Club Plaza opened to critical acclaim, Nichols was eager to recommend Delk, along with landscape architect Hare & Hare Company, to his friend Waite Phillips. (Coincidentally, a later philanthropist for Philmont, Norman Clapp, also gained notoriety by building an early suburban shopping center, in Washington state).

After the Waite Phillips Company was sold on July 25, 1925, the man for which it was named had time and energy to pour into the Villa projects. Ned Delk came to Cimarron that October to survey the grounds of the old Urraca Ranch apple orchard, where the Villa would showcase a majestic view of the mountains to the west. Delk executed an initial architectural sketch. Blueprints were finalized in early 1926, and construction commenced at a fast and furious pace. As building continued by the John Long Company at both the New Mexico and Oklahoma projects, the Phillips family (minus youngster Chope, who stayed at Philmont) boarded an ocean liner in June and sailed for Europe.

The brilliant courtyard was originally a swimming pool. (Photo by Matthew Prokosch, Philmont News and Photo Services)

The holiday provided inspiration for Waite and Genevieve for style and furnishings for the burgeoning residences back in the states. Designers and builders were required to make changes on the fly, and Waite Phillips was actively involved in all his construction projects.

The Long Company completed the Villa Philmonte in the spring of 1927, and the Phillips family took residence that June, shortly after the Villa Philbrook had been christened with a house-warming party that was the buzz of Tulsa society. The opening of the Villa Philmonte was much lower key. Waite brought out his four brothers, Frank, L. E., Ed, and Fred, to celebrate the Fourth of July and bask in the cool New Mexican climate.

The Philbrook in Tulsa was considered a masterpiece, though some critics hailed it as ostentatious, over the top. It was built at a price tag of $1.1 million. The one-third smaller Philmonte, built in a Spanish Mediterranean style in contrast to the former's Italian Renaissance design, also earned praise for its architecture, setting, and tasteful furnishing.

Clearly, Waite and Genevieve Phillips were happy with their new homes. Architect Delk was promptly

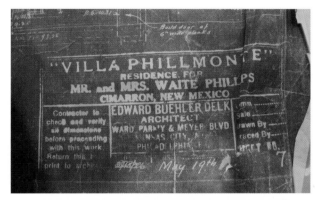

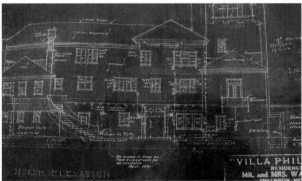

The Philmont Museum recently acquired the original blueprints of Edward Buehler Delk from the successor of his Kansas City architectural firm. (Photos by author David Mullings)

assigned to design a twenty-three-story commercial building in downtown Tulsa. It would become Philtower, and was later included in the second Philmont gift to the Boy Scouts.

The Villa's living room.

Stairs lead from the main floor to the New Mexico Room and auto court.

Stained-glass windows depict a scene of the coming of the Santa Fe Trail onto the New Mexico plains.

The sunny solarium sits south of the master bedroom.

With twenty-two rooms, the Villa Philmonte is centered around the large living room, featuring massive ceiling beams, a large fireplace, and a grand player piano. To its south sits a sunny solarium with an ornate fountain. A long hallway, with four vaulted ceiling sections, leads from the living room to the dining room.

A stained-glass window highlights a landing between the Villa's first and second floors. Its scene depicts Indians looking on as pioneers pass into the territory on the Santa Fe Trail. At the top of the stairs, the library and its porthole window face toward the mountains to the west. The bedrooms of the Phillips kids, Helen Jane and Chope, are found on the north side of the second floor, while Waite's and Genevieve's quarters are to the south, including his and hers dressing rooms. The pink-tiled master bathroom is noted for its heat lamps, temperature gauge, and seven-head shower. The downstairs of the Villa takes on a decidedly masculine tone; Waite Phillips

The tastefully appointed dining room.

enjoyed working and entertaining there. An entrance from the auto court and garages leads to the Trophy Room, adorned with heads of game harvested from the ranch, and the New Mexico Room, site of a Fourth of July poker game among the Phillips brothers where they carved their initials into a table.

Across one of two patios to the east of what has become affectionately known as "The Big House" is situated a two-story guesthouse. The northern patio leads to what was the Villa's swimming pool, but was converted to a flower garden in the 1950s.

The Boy Scouts of America has taken care to preserve its unique asset. The Villa Philmonte was used early on for Philmont Training Center functions, and it remains central to modern training activity. Two major restoration and preservation projects have helped keep the Villa Philmonte as it was for the fourteen years that it was occupied by the Phillips family. In 1976, Chope Phillips and his wife Virginia led an effort to restore the Villa to its original appearance, utilizing photographs taken in the 1930s. Then, over a five-year period from 2000 to 2005, the Villa underwent three phases of improvement at a cost of $1.45 million. First, the electrical, plumbing, and heating systems were overhauled. The second phase involved rebuilding walkways and fountains around the Villa, including making the dramatic mountain lion vertical fountain operational again. Lastly, in 2005, the Villa's roof was restored and new copper gutters were installed.

Today, 15,000 to 18,000 people tour the Villa Philmonte each year, gaining a glimpse into the life and times of Waite Phillips and his family.

NO BUFFALO

Waite Phillips wasn't ready for highest Boy Scout award

The Boy Scouts of America's Silver Buffalo Award honors, at the national level, its high-level leaders and supporters who have demonstrated extraordinary service to youth.

It may seem curious that Waite Phillips is not on the list of about 700 leaders who have been so honored over the past eight decades. His omission is not because Phillips was not asked to receive the award. He was, twice. And twice, he declined.

On the second instance, in May 1950, Phillips explained that he thought any award to be premature. From the archives of his correspondence: "With all due regard for the generous thought of you three gentlemen," he wrote to BSA President Walter Head, "I prefer to wait until proof is established that an award of merit for it has been earned. This will not be true regarding me until such time as my original plan has been brought to maturity for making boy scouts and their adult leaders the sole beneficiaries of this enterprise, and that can only become effective when their transportation charges and camping fees to Philmont are reduced to a minimum."

Head replied: "It will be a source of keen disappointment… that you still feel impelled to decline the Silver Buffalo Award, which all of us have long felt should be bestowed upon you in recognition of your outstanding contribution to the Boy Scout movement in America."

Even with Phillips's two-time rejection, the Phillips family has two Silver Buffaloes to its credit. Waite's older brother, Frank, an early and enthusiastic Scouting supporter and likely influence on his younger sibling, was given his award in 1942. Waite's son Elliot "Chope" was recognized in 1998 for his cowboy-boots-on-the-ground role in helping to carry out his father's vision for Philmont.

Ernest Thompson Seton, namesake of the library at the Philmont Museum, was in the 1926 inaugural class of Silver Buffalo Award recipients. The following year, Walter Head would be honored, a decade before he would play a key role in the transfer of Philmont from Phillips to the Boy Scouts. Head had

Waite Phillips, left, stands with the Foyt couple and Arthur Schuck, the chief Scout executive when Philmont was donated to the Boy Scouts of America.

A Silver Buffalo Award—among the first—given to Ernest Thompson Seton is displayed at the Philmont Museum, in the library named for him.

suggested that it would be appropriate for Waite Phillips and Arthur Schuck, the chief Scout executive during the Philmont donation period, to be given awards in the same year. Indeed, Schuck did get his honor in 1950.

Norton Clapp, a Seattle business executive and longtime prominent Scouter, received a Silver Buffalo in 1954, nearly a decade before he financed the Philmont purchase of the Baldy country.

CHOPE

Waite's only son inspired gift, helped Philmont develop

Perhaps without Waite Phillips's only son, there might not have been Philmont Scout Ranch. During a horseback ride to the Rayado Lodge at Fish Camp with an early Philmont general manager, Waite Phillips said, "You may wonder why I've disposed of the Philmont Ranch by giving it to the Boy Scouts. Our son, Elliot, and his cousins have enjoyed the ranch and I want many other boys to have the same experience."

Even as a skinny youngster, Elliot Phillips took to the outdoors and didn't really care for city life or material things. After his father acquired his northern New Mexico acreage, his only son took to the cowboy life quickly, becoming a real ranch hand, even if a diminutive one. Older cousins doing summer work started calling Elliot "Shorty," then a longtime Philmont cowboy named Malaquias Espinoza branded him with the nickname that would stay with him for the rest of his life. "Chopo" is Spanish slang for "shorty."

Waite Phillips had designs that Chope follow in his footsteps as an oilman and businessman. Chope gave

Young Elliot "Chope" Phillips was always at home in the saddle. (Courtesy of the Philmont Museum archives)

Instead of joining the rest of his family on a European tour in the summer of 1926, teenaged Chope chose to be a young cowboy at Philmont. Here, an even younger Chope (back to the camera) helps in branding at the La Grulla camp. (Courtesy of the Philmont Museum archives)

it a shot, working for a couple of years in the Kansas oilfields. But Chope's heart was on the New Mexican ranch lands, and his place was in the saddle.

In his early twenties, he watched with disappointment as his father gave away the ranch he had grown up on and loved, and then sold off the last southern portion. Years later, Waite would buy Chope and his wife Virginia an 18,000-acre ranch at Watrous, New Mexico, some sixty miles south of Philmont, which Chope said "was all that I ever wanted." Unlike his father, Chope was no gentleman rancher. He worked his ranch, hard.

Though Chope was no longer a Philmont cowboy, he remained a frequent visitor, member of the Philmont Ranch Committee, and active supporter of the Boy Scout program. Chope and Virginia created a foundation with the substantial inheritance left to them by Genevieve Phillips. Philmont has been a benefactor of sometimes large grants from that fund. In 1998, Chope Phillips was awarded Scouting's highest adult leadership honor, the Silver Buffalo.

And the Phillips connection continues. Julie Puckett, Chope's daughter, serves on the Ranch Committee, and her daughter Lelah—Chope's granddaughter and Waite's great-granddaughter— served on the Philmont staff in 2012 and 2013.

Chope and his wife Virginia, pictured here in the summer of 1979, at his mother Genevieve's ninety-second birthday party.

CHAPTER 4
75 YEARS OF SCOUTING

TIMELINE

Steady progress at Philmont seen over seventy-five years

1938: Waite and Genevieve Phillips donate 35,857 acres of their New Mexico ranch, Philmont, to the Boy Scouts of America. It will be called Philturn Rockymountain Scoutcamp. The deed was signed on November 28; seventy-five years later, that was Thanksgiving Day, about the time this book went to the publisher.

1939: Philturn opens, hosting 189 participants. Each camper receives a Philturn "Silver Dollar" patch.

1941: The Waite Phillips family donates an additional 91,538 acres including the Villa Philmonte to the BSA. Philturn Rockymountain Scoutcamp becomes Philmont Scout Ranch.

1942: First official season as Philmont Scout Ranch. A total of 275 participants attend and earn the Philmont Silver Dollar patch. An Army Air Force B-24 bomber crashes into Trail Peak.

1943: Horses and cattle are branded with the "new" Philmont brands.

1945: The "Diamond Hitch" finance course begins being taught at Philmont. Order of the Arrow founder E. Urner Goodman visits Philmont.

1946: The first red wool shirts with a black bull over the left pocket are presented to twelve BSA regional executives.

1947: Dr. Ray "Doc" Loomis attends Philmont. He becomes known nationwide for teaching camping skills, Dutch oven cooking, and the proper use of the axe.

1948: William "Green Bar Bill" Hillcourt gives the first Woodbadge course at Philmont.

1950: The Philmont Training Center officially opens.

1951: Segment awards are added to the Silver Dollar patch. Each segment represents a different skill or program completed.

1956: Twelve-day treks become the standard.

1957: The Ranger program is formed. The first Philmont Arrowhead patch is awarded.

1960: Clear Creek Mountain, the highest peak on Philmont at the time, is renamed Waite Phillips Mountain.

1961: By this time, 100,000 Scouts have hiked at Philmont.

1963: Norton Clapp donates 10,098 acres, which include the 12,441-foot peak of Baldy Mountain.

A state historical sign at Ponil marks the beginnings of the Boy Scouts on what would become Philmont Scout Ranch. (Photo by author David Mullings)

1967: The Philmont Museum and Seton Memorial Library opens.

1971: The Conservation Department is formed.

1973: The search and rescue team PhilSAR is officially organized.

1985: The first official *Philmont Field Guide* is published. The first Order of Arrow course is taught at Philmont.

1988: Philmont celebrates its fiftieth anniversary. By this time, 500,000 Scouts have hiked on Philmont. "Two Deep Leadership" is implemented by BSA.

1992: Pennzoil donates 100,000 acres to the U.S. Forest Service, allowing one-fourth of Philmont's summer participants to hike and camp in the neighboring Carson National Forest.

1993: *Tyrannosaurus rex*'s foot track is discovered in the North Ponil Canyon. It is the first *T. rex* track ever authenticated.

2000: Philmont celebrates the millennium with a special "P2K" edition of the Arrowhead patch.

2002: The Ponil Complex Fire occurs. About 28,000 acres of Philmont's north country are ravaged by wildfire. Before the fire is contained it will burn 90,000 acres and become New Mexico's largest fire on record.

2010: The one-hundredth anniversary of BSA. Philmont commemorates this milestone with a special "BSA 100" edition of the Arrowhead patch.

2013: Philmont celebrates its seventy-fifth anniversary.

2014: ONE MILLION Scouts will have hiked on Philmont!

EARLY SCOUTING DAYS

*Popularity grew as program
experiments took hold*

After the Phillipses' twin donations, it took the Boy Scouts several years to settle on an ideal core program. In 1956, they found it—the twelve-day trek, with eleven on the trail.

The early years, after the 1938 and 1941 gifts, saw Philmont experiment with a smattering of programs, and even none at all. When the Philturn Rockymountain Scoutcamp hosted its first visitors in 1939, the groups of senior Scouts (minimum age was fifteen years) were allowed to make their own itineraries. They could backpack during their entire trip, mix in horse and burro packing activities, and even take side day-trips to regional attractions, such as the Taos Pueblo or the Capulin Volcano.

After Philturn became Philmont and World War II ended, Philmont's Senior Training program blossomed, and the activities it offered became the precursor to the twelve-day treks among backcountry camps with their themed programs. Senior Training, which aimed to teach older Scouts outdoor skills they could share with their home troops, taught its participants during their first week skills such as horsemanship, nature study, cooking, packing, marksmanship, and others. A second week was split between burro packing and backpacking.

Other early "schedules" instituted under Camping Director George Bullock included the Wagon Train program (much the same as Senior Training, but a

Burros have always been a central part of the Philmont outdoor experience. (Courtesy of the Philmont Museum archives)

Scouts take to the trail in the early days, bearing backpacks a little primitive by today's standards. (Courtesy of the Philmont Museum archives)

A Scout shows off a Boy Scout uniform, circa 1939. (Courtesy of the Philmont Museum archives)

Beasts of burden help Scouts get to the next camp. (Courtesy of the Philmont Museum archives)

full twenty-three days), the Service Corps (two weeks of trail building and conservation projects), the Cavalcade (six days on horseback), the Kit Carson Trek (all backpacking, and climbing of Philmont's highest five peaks), the Junior Leader Training Troop (a month learning teaching techniques), and the Ranch Pioneering Trek (thirty days, much like the Service Corps).

Philmont, with its unique outdoor programs, was a hit. By the mid-1950s, summer attendance had grown from the mere hundreds of the first few years to about 8,000. That volume of Scouts started to

create logistical difficulties with the existing lineup of schedules. Jack Rhea, who took over as Camping Director in 1954, made a big change in 1956. He standardized all prior programs into the trek system still used today—the twelve-day High Adventure Expedition that allows crews to pick the terrain they cross and the activities found at chosen camps. That summer, Philmont attendance topped 10,000 for the first time.

The following year, Rhea and legendary camp-craft instructor Doc Loomis started another now-standard Philmont practice, sending a staff

Religion is, and has been, best practiced out-of-doors at Philmont. (Courtesy of the Philmont Museum archives)

If it's been built at Philmont—be it cabin or trail—chances are youngsters have lent a helping hand. (Courtesy of the Philmont Museum archives)

The old Aztec mine became part of Philmont's program in 1967 when Ray Bryan and Matt Gorman, a former Aztec superintendent, sawed an aspen log in half at an opening ceremony.

member "ranger" out with a crew for the trek's first six days to offer advice and ensure the Scouts were equipped to negotiate the terrain on their own for the final six days. The time a ranger spent on the trail was whittled down to four days in 1960, then two in 1962; today it is three, with two on the trail.

The early twelve-day treks served Philmont and its visiting Scouts well, but the system was not perfect. Bottlenecks would develop at certain camps, as crews could choose their own itineraries, and because Philmont's growing popularity increased trail traffic. Into the 1960s, 400 campers could be found on Cimarroncito on a given night. Or Beaubien, with the 1965 flood having washed away many campsites at Fish Camp, would see a crowd of 300. Additionally, crew-planned itineraries often resulted in logistical headaches, including poorly-thought-out food drops, bad sequences of camps with no water or no facilities, and ill-timed bus transportation.

In 1968, a record 18,648 Scouts flocked to Philmont, tipping the scales. The next summer Philmont implemented pre-planned itineraries, where the Scout Ranch dictated routes from which visiting crews could choose. The added organization and traffic control have allowed Philmont to host an average of 17,275 trekkers since the change was adopted. Attendance has been more than 20,000 each summer since 2002, including a record 23,325 in 2012.

One early "schedule" at Philmont was the Cavalcade, six days out on horseback. (Courtesy of the Philmont Museum archives)

Many have shaped Philmont; here are ten

Over its first seventy-five years, Philmont has seen many great visionaries, leaders, and high-spirited hard workers who have helped meld the ranch into the world-class facility it is today. In no particular order, here are ten men who left large footprints at Philmont, with apologies to the other ten, twenty, or fifty who are deserving of inclusion. Much of the background of these men was drawn from Minor Huffman's book, *High Adventure Among the Magic Mountains: Philmont the First 50 Years.*

George Bullock

George Bullock. World War II, which started just as Philmont was being created, stunted the Scout Ranch's early growth because of transportation limitations and manpower needed in local war efforts. The conflict's end in 1945 meant Philmont was ready to really get started. The man selected to guide the ranch through its early expansion was a native Texan named George Bullock. He took over as program director in 1947. Bullock created the trekking schedules and back-country-themed activities that remain the core of the Philmont experience. Back then, the schedules

Boss Sanchez

were known as the Wagon Train, the Expedition, the Cavalcade, the Kit Carson Trek, Junior Leader Training, and Explorer Encampment. Bullock also started a program to recognize Scouts for learning outdoor skills in horsemanship, conservation, camping, and nature. During Bullock's tenure, Kit Carson's adobe home at Rayado was reconstructed. Attendance in Bullock's final year as program manager, 1954, was just shy of 8,000 Scouts, more than four times that of 1947, when he took the job.

Lawrence "Boss" Sanchez. Sanchez, the longtime head of the ranch's Horse Department, earned his nickname in the 1940s when the ranch foreman asked him to temporarily supervise a fence crew. The other men jokingly started calling him "Boss." But Sanchez lived up to the moniker when, in 1954, he was moved from assistant to head wrangler of a department key to the Philmont program and operation. He would hold the job for twenty-nine years until his retirement in 1983. Sanchez was first hired as a cowboy in 1941, shortly before the second Waite Phillips donation. The Scout Ranch's first

Joe Davis   Jack Rhea

Philmont Director of Camping Joe Davis enjoys the summit of Baldy Mountain with a crew in the late 1960s.

general manager, Minor Huffman, said Sanchez's steady hand with the horses was invaluable to the new Scout managers. "We always said he came with the big gift," Huffman wrote.

Joe Davis. A firmer-than-firm handshake, boundless optimism, a booming voice, and the hearty admonition to "carry on!" were the hallmarks of this camping director who served a decade starting in 1965. His first days on the job saw Davis having to deal with a challenging emergency—the historic Flood of 1965. Under his guidance, the summer season was delayed but one week. Davis would go on during his tenure to implement many innovations, including improved staff training, opening the program to young ladies, the strenuous Kit Carson Men program, and a study of the impact of the high number of Scouts on Philmont's wilderness. However, Davis was perhaps best known for his intense, caring person-to-person relations with each Scout or ranger he met. After Davis died in 2008 at age ninety-six, these were some of the comments made by former Philmonters: "It will be a long time before we have another who makes Joe's kind of impact." "He treated me as a man, not a child." "He was the most positive-thinking and uplifting person I have ever or will ever meet."

Jack Rhea. Under Rhea's seven-year watch as director of camping, the ranger program was instituted and the standard twelve-day trek replaced the Expeditions and Cavalcades. Beginning in 1957, a Philmont ranger would accompany visiting crews for six of their twelve days on the trail, ensuring the trekkers had the necessary education and skills to go it alone. Also in 1957, Philmont's Volunteer Training Center shifted into a higher gear, adding its two tent cities to accommodate a higher number of adult leaders and their families.

Mark Anderson. The long-tenured director of program has seen and met the challenge of guiding Philmont's core program into the computer and smartphone ages. Anderson took over the top program position (and with it, residence in the old Ladd home) in 1999 and remained on the job as Philmont celebrated its seventy-fifth anniversary in 2013 and beyond. Anderson maintained the forward-thinking innovation of his predecessors. The achievements under his watch include using the ranch as the stage for more than twenty research projects in fields ranging from botany to geology to wildlife. Researchers from Stanford and Northwestern universities have been counted among the collaborators on these projects. In the most recent decade, Philmont has adopted a "best practices" approach to natural resource

Mark Anderson

Steve Zimmer

Bill Littrell

management and been receptive to a variety of technology opportunities, such as partnering with a defense contractor to provide a "bare earth" analysis of ranch acreage.

Stephen Zimmer. The Philmont Museum and Seton Memorial Library are considered the education center and the conscience of the Scout Ranch. A man central to the facility's growth and success and to chronicling the ranch history was Steve Zimmer. Despite suffering from polio as a youth, Zimmer worked at Philmont for three years in the early 1970s, and then signed on as a staff member at the museum in 1976. By 1980, he was promoted to museum director, a post he held for the next twenty-one years. After writing several books on Philmont and Cimarron-area history, Zimmer can be considered the foremost expert on the interpretation of Philmont, and the history of the area and its people. Over the decades, Zimmer has lived the cowboy life from his family spread in nearby Miami, east of Rayado.

Bill Littrell. William C. Littrell was noted as the first general manager at Philmont not to come from the professional ranks of Scouting. He held the top job from 1974 to 1976. However, his biggest impact at Philmont came during the twenty years he served as farm and ranch superintendent, from 1954 to 1974. Philmont, of course, is and always has been a working

Bill Littrell, Ray Bryan, and Jack Rhea.

(and profitable) ranch, but one with the added goal of exposing young Scouts to the ways of livestock and agriculture. By all accounts, Littrell was successful. Philmont earned several awards from ranching organizations for its practices, and was known for the high quality of its Hereford cattle. Prior to his Philmont years, Littrell grew up on a ranch near Maxwell and Springer and earned a degree in agriculture at New Mexico State University.

Ned Gold Jr. Philmont would not be Philmont without the incredible employees who have kept it firing on all cylinders for seventy-five years. The magical Philmont experience has understandably created strong bonds among the folks who have toiled there. Ned Gold first dreamed up the idea for the organization of the Philmont fraternity in 1963, when he was director of the Lost Cabin Trail Camp. Gold worked at Philmont for two more years and then wrote the first proposal for the Philmont Staff Association in 1966. Seven years later, the non-profit association was incorporated. Gold was elected its first president, from 1976 to 1978. For forty years, the PSA has reunited staff members, promoting equal doses of camaraderie and service. In 2013, Philmont christened the "Ned Gold Room" for meetings and conferences in the new Hardesty Casa Central building.

Minor Huffman

Ned Gold Jr.

Ray Bryan

Minor Huffman. Once Waite Phillips dropped an unbelievable chunk of land in the lap of the Boy Scouts of America, somebody had to get the place going. He was Minor Huffman, the only man to serve simultaneously as Philmont's general manager and director of program, which he did in 1944. Coming shortly on the heels of the big Phillips donation, Huffman arrived during a transitional period where Philmont was inventing itself. By the time Huffman finished his three-year stint as general manager in 1946, Philmont had become established as more than just an ordinary Boy Scout camp, and the foundation had been laid for its adult leadership training program. Huffman wasn't done with Scouting or Philmont, though. He continued on for eighteen years as Scout executive for the second-largest council in the country, the Sam Houston Area. Then in 1988, for Philmont's fiftieth, he wrote and published *High Adventure Among the Magic Mountains*, preserving valuable details from the early days from a key player's perspective.

Ray Bryan. Bryan was among five Boy Scouting officials dispatched to Philmont in October 1938 to check out the Ponil property being offered as a gift by Waite Phillips. Once it was accepted, Bryan, a member of the national staff in the Engineering Department, was sent back to supervise construction of the Ponil Lodge and other buildings and facilities needed to make the Philturn Rockymountain Scoutcamp fully functional. For Bryan, it would be the start of a long and productive Philmont connection. After a year supervising the Boy Scouts' Third National Jamboree, Bryan was appointed to Philmont's top job, general manager of Philmont properties, which included the Philtower building in Tulsa. He would serve in that capacity for sixteen years, by far the longest tenured at that job. Under Bryan's watch, Philmont began to study its growing popularity and realize that it was putting its resources at risk of overuse.

PHILMONT EXPANDS

Baldy gift made in 1963 by secondary benefactor Clapp

Waite and Genevieve Phillips were not the only benefactors of land that comprises Philmont Scout Ranch.

Philmont, as it has been for the last fifty years, came together as three gifts. The first two, of course, were made by the Phillips family; the north Ponil-Philturn tract of 35,857 acres in 1938, followed in 1941 by the stunning bequeathing of the central and southern parts of the ranch, including the Villa Philmonte and headquarters area. The additional 91,538 acres brought the Scout Ranch to its expansive size of 127,395 acres.

But something was missing. It was the last remaining piece of the original Maxwell Land Grant, encompassing Old Baldy Mountain, the sentinel of the mountains between Cimarron and the Moreno Valley.

In 1963, twenty-five years after the Phillipses' initial gift, a business executive and philanthropist from Washington state, Norton Clapp, provided $196,520 in financing so that Philmont could purchase 10,098 acres of rugged land on the east flank of Baldy Mountain.

Clapp's life shared many parallels with that of Waite Phillips. Clapp was an extraordinarily industrious and energetic man, suffered from family tragedy, shared his time and money for numerous charitable causes, and capitalized greatly on family business connections. When Clapp was thirteen and growing up in California, his mother was killed in an automobile accident. Clapp would go on to survive the death of one wife and a son in another auto crash, a second wife's death in a plane crash, and the loss of two sons to cancer.

Above: Philmont Camping Director Joe Davis supervises the setting of a plaque commemorating Norton Clapp's financial contribution that enabled Philmont to acquire the Baldy country. (Courtesy of the Philmont Museum archives)

Left: Norton Clapp eventually served as president of the Boy Scouts of America. (Courtesy of the Philmont Museum archives)

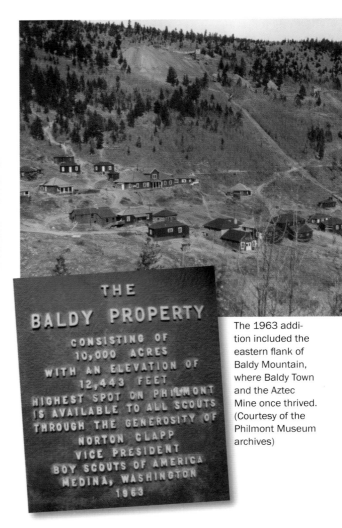

The 1963 addition included the eastern flank of Baldy Mountain, where Baldy Town and the Aztec Mine once thrived. (Courtesy of the Philmont Museum archives)

Early in his career Clapp was a lawyer and developer, responsible for building one of the first suburban shopping centers west of the Mississippi River, the Lakewood Colonial Center near Tacoma in 1937. Later, he was one of five men who stepped up to build the Space Needle in Seattle for the 1962 World's Fair, after public financing failed.

Two of Clapp's maternal ancestors were lumbermen in Minnesota who went on to provide backing to Frederick Weyerhaeuser in 1900, for an ambitious timber enterprise in the northwestern United States. Weyerhaeuser's group bought 900,000 acres of timberland from the Northern Pacific Railway. Clapp worked a stint as Weyerhaeuser's corporate

secretary in the late 1930s, but with the onset of World War II, enlisted in Navy. He again became involved with the corporation in 1946, succeeding his late father as a director on the firm's board. In 1960, he became Weyerhaeuser's president, overseeing a global expansion and rise in profitability for the lumber company over six years. Clapp remained as the board's chairman until 1976.

In Scouting, Clapp started as a Scoutmaster in Lakewood and then served in several volunteer council and regional capacities. He was on the Boy Scouts' National Executive Board for several decades and was president of the national organization from 1971 to 1973. He claimed to have flown a quarter of a million miles on Boy Scout business.

Clapp died in 1995 at age eighty-seven. *Fortune* magazine reported he was worth $450 million at the time, making him one of the richest people in America.

The acreage added by Clapp's donation gave Philmont Scouts access to the historic gold mining territory, including the Aztec Mine, which had yielded more than $4 million worth of gold in the nineteenth century. It also included the ranch's new high point, Old Baldy Mountain.

PHILMONT FORTNIGHT

NASA astronauts learned geology on a two-week seminar

Twelve men, just twelve, have set foot on Earth's moon. And just twelve others have ever escaped the orbital bounds of the planet, making the trip around the lunar satellite. All twenty-four, of course, were astronauts in the National Aeronautical and Space Administration, during NASA's glory moon years from 1968 through 1972.

Interestingly, Philmont Scout Ranch played a role in their journeys, and in winning the Space Race. President Kennedy in May 1961 told a joint session of Congress: "I believe that this nation should commit itself to achieving the goal, before this decade is out, of landing a man on the moon and returning him safely to the earth." With the Soviet Union as the other entrant in the race, and with the USSR claiming the launch of the first person into space, NASA went all in with its Gemini, then Apollo programs.

Three Mays after Kennedy laid down the challenge, NASA sent a group of astronauts to Philmont for training in geological mapping and seismographic study, all in anticipation of landing a manned U.S. craft on the moon. Historical records of how many astronauts participated are conflicting. A group photograph shot at the end of the session shows

Charles Pillmore, USGS geologist, shows astronaut Elliot See, center, how to use the Jacobs Staff while astronaut Dick Gordon makes strike and dip measurements. (NASA official photograph, courtesy of the Philmont Museum archives)

Astronauts pose in their new red Philmont jacks gifted to them. The Eagle Scouts among them lined up front and center, and in light-colored pants. (NASA official photograph, courtesy of the Philmont Museum archives)

Astronauts Charles Conrad and Gene Cernan, foreground, locate position by resection. (NASA official photograph, courtesy of the Philmont Museum archives)

twenty astronauts. A book written on Philmont's fiftieth anniversary reported that twenty-nine astronauts came to Philmont, and that only the thirtieth, John Glenn, did not attend. But in a thank-you note sent to Philmont by astronaut Alan Bean, he three times refers to himself as writing on behalf of "the fourteen." It might be surmised that the latter number engaged in intensive training, while the others may have been on hand for only a portion of the studies. For instance, Neil Armstrong is shown in the group-of-twenty photograph and in NASA pictures shot in the Philmont field, but is not listed as one of "the fourteen."

During two weeks in the spring of 1964 at Philmont, the NASA crew was put up at the Volunteer Training Center at the Villa Philmonte. It was not a leisurely stay. The astronauts arose early, had breakfast, and took to the field for a full day. Most field operations were conducted just a stone's throw northwest from Philmont's headquarters, on Horse Ridge, just east of Webster Reservoir and above Cimarroncito Creek. After dinner, they continued studies, recorded that day's work, and planned for the next day's curriculum. One can

imagine camaraderie among the astronauts and team-building were part of the collateral benefit of the NASA academic mission—the same benefits experienced by young Scouts on the same site.

On their last day, the astronauts were feted with some Philmont food and entertainment. Staff and neighboring residents got to mingle and meet an already legendary group of aviators, including several who would go on after the moonshots to become household names.

These were the six astronauts who hit the rocks at Philmont in 1964, then went on to dig the rocks while scampering on the moon.

Neil Armstrong. On July 21, 1969, Neil Armstrong proclaimed, "That's one small step for [a] man, one giant leap for mankind." He is prominently featured in NASA's photos of the Philmont visit. In his youth, Armstrong attained the Eagle Scout award. On his way to the moon on *Apollo 11* in 1969, he took time to greet "my fellow Scouts and Scouters" at the National Jamboree in Idaho. The first man on the moon died at age eighty-two in August 2012.

Buzz Aldrin. Armstrong's lunar module partner Edwin Eugene "Buzz" Aldrin's mother's maiden name was—imagine this—Moon. Aldrin was supposedly the second man on the moon only because of the physical positioning of the pair in the tight module.

Pete Conrad. Pete Conrad commanded *Apollo 12* and became the third man to make lunar footprints. "Whoopee! Man, that may have been a small one for Neil, but that's a long one for me," he proclaimed. Conrad went on to command the first manned Skylab space station mission.

Alan Bean. Having grown up in the Texas panhandle, Alan Bean at Philmont was not far from home. After *Apollo 12* was hit by lightning just seconds into its launch in late 1969, Bean performed the operation that restored telemetry and salvaged the moon flight. Bean sat next to Conrad when *Apollo 12*'s lunar module touched down on November 19.

David Scott. Commander of *Apollo 15*, David Scott became the seventh on the moon. It was his third space flight following *Gemini 8* (with Armstrong) and *Apollo 9*, which demonstrated the viability of docking the command and lunar modules. Scott's Philmont training was put to use, as *Apollo 15* gathered a record 180 pounds of lunar material. Scott and James Irwin spent about eighteen hours roving the moon over three days.

Eugene Cernan. An alumnus of Purdue University like Armstrong, Cernan holds the distinction of being the last man to be on the moon (at least for a long while). He commanded *Apollo 17*, but perhaps his finest hour was as lunar module pilot on *Apollo 10*, the dress rehearsal for Armstrong's and Aldrin's great adventure. Cernan piloted *10*'s lunar module to within eight miles of the lunar surface.

This list highlights Philmont-trained astronauts who made it to the moon, but only in orbit, not to the surface.

Michael Collins. Originally assigned to *Apollo 9*, Michael Collins suffered medical problems that got him bumped... to the historic flight of *Apollo 11*. He was the third wheel left behind in the command module as Armstrong and Aldrin made history below, but showed no regret. "This venture has been structured for three men, and I consider my third as necessary as either of the other two." On the dark side of each orbit, Collins was out of contact with Earth for forty-eight minutes. Was he lonely? On the contrary. His mindset was one of "awareness, anticipation, satisfaction, confidence, almost exultation."

Dick Gordon. Dick Gordon followed Collins's lead, and was command module pilot for *Apollo 12*. Tabbed as commander of *Apollo 18*, he was slated

to walk on the moon before the flight was scuttled because of budget cuts.

Jim Lovell. Jim Lovell grew up in Milwaukee, made Eagle Scout, earned Scouting's highest adult honor—the Silver Buffalo—in 1992, and served as president of the National Eagle Scout Association. So the time spent at Philmont in 1964 must have been special for him. On *Apollo 8*, Lovell served as navigator for the first manned flight to moon. With Borman and Anders, the crew entered lunar orbit on Christmas Eve, 1968, headed back Earthbound on Christmas Day. Lovell was to walk on the moon on his second venture there, on *Apollo 13*, in April 1970. But before the craft got there, an oxygen tank burst, putting the mission, crew, and craft in great peril. Tom Hanks famously played Lovell in *Apollo 13*, which described the drama of the amazing recovery mission.

Space flight and exploration is dangerous business, and nearly a quarter of the astronauts who trained at Philmont met an early, tragic demise.

Roger Chaffee. The Naval aviator was an avid hunter, and he must have had thoughts beyond mere geology while at Philmont. Roger Chaffee, an Eagle Scout, never made it into space, but died in a horrific fire in *Apollo 1* as it sat on the launch pad at Cape Kennedy on January 27, 1967.

Ed White. "I'm coming back in, and it's the saddest moment of my life." That's what Ed White said as he ended the first-ever spacewalk by an American. That was off *Gemini 4*, of which he was the pilot. White died with Chaffee and Gus Grissom in the *Apollo 1* tragedy.

Theodore Freeman. Just five short months after his time at Philmont, Theodore Freeman became the first astronaut to suffer a flight-related death. A bird strike caused the crash of his training jet on an Air Force base in Texas. Freeman was thirty-four.

Charles Bassett. Charles Bassett was an active Boy Scout in Ohio, reaching the rank of Life Scout. He was regarded as one of the most capable of the astronauts of the time, and was assigned with Elliot See to *Gemini 9*.

Elliot See. This Eagle Scout was flying with Bassett in their T-38 training jet to St. Louis, where they were to train on a *Gemini* simulator. The weather at Lambert Field was bad, and on a second approach, the plane came in too low. The plane crashed into the McDonnell Space Center. The wreckage came to rest less than 500 feet from the *Gemini* spacecraft the pair were to fly.

C. C. Williams. A Marine Corps major, C. C. Williams became the third astronaut to die in a NASA T-38 jet trainer, on October 5, 1967. He was on his way to Alabama to see his dying father. Williams could have been on track to fly on *Apollo 12*.

Edward Givens. Another Life Scout at Philmont, Edward Givens never got a chance to fly. He was on the support crew of *Apollo 7*, but died in a car crash near the Houston Space Center.

Here's how the future played out for the other astronauts who trained at Philmont that spring.

Donn Eisele. Donn Eisele, former Eagle Scout, piloted the command module on *Apollo 7*, the first manned flight of the third generation of American rocket ships.

Gordon Cooper. Gordon "Gordo" Cooper was a Boy Scout in Oklahoma, reaching Life Scout rank. He had already been in space, on *Mercury-Atlas 9*, exactly a year earlier than when he arrived with his colleagues at Philmont. The sixth American in orbit, he logged more time in space than the previous five combined. In August 1965, Cooper and Conrad proved astronauts could survive in space long enough to get to the moon and back. They logged 120 orbits over eight days. Cooper had a falling out with NASA leadership and retired in 1970.

Rusty Schweickart. Rusty Schweickart flew on *Apollo 9*, just months before *11*, and performed the first *Apollo* spacewalk. He suffered from space sickness, though, and didn't fly again.

William Anders. On *Apollo 8*, William Anders along with Borman and Lovell became the first humans to leave the bounds of Earth's gravity and see the far side of the moon. They were named *TIME*'s Men of the Year for 1968. While orbiting the moon, Anders took an iconic photo, "Earthrise." *Apollo 8* was the only space flight for Anders, a Life Scout. After his time at NASA, he held many prominent government and business positions.

Walter Cunningham. Walter Cunningham was born in Creston, Iowa, where Waite Phillips's older brother Frank first was an entrepreneur. On *Apollo 8*, the first flight after the *Apollo 1* disaster, Cunningham took the lunar module pilot seat. The mission succeeded, but none of the crew flew again because of friction with on-ground command.

A trio of footnotes can be added to the astronauts-at-Philmont story. Among experts working with the astronauts was U.S. Geological Service geologist Charles Pillmore, who would go on to discover the first-ever footprint of a *Tyrannosaurus rex* on north Philmont land. Little did either Pillmore or Neil Armstrong know as they worked together in that spring of 1964 that one would be the first human to set foot on a sphere other than our Earth, and that the other would make a landmark discovery of a creature who set foot on Philmont country tens of millions of years ago.

Also, Philmont's iconic Arrowhead patch has made it into space. Astronaut Michael Fossum, an Eagle Scout who hiked the ranch, carried one on his flight aboard the space shuttle *Discovery* in 2006. He gave the keynote speech at Philmont's opening staff meeting the following year.

Lastly, the twelfth of the twelve men to set foot on the moon, Harrison Schmitt, was not among the astronauts at Philmont. But as a native New Mexican and a professional geologist, Schmitt would have been right at home and in his element during the NASA Philmont fortnight. He was recruited in 1965 with the first group of citizen astronauts. Like Glenn in Ohio, Schmitt became a U.S. senator, from New Mexico, though he served just one term. The opponent who defeated him campaigned on a slogan, "What on Earth have you done for me lately?"

NATURE'S WRATH

Scout Ranch copes with disasters, accidents

In Philmont's mountains, Mother Nature reveals all her splendors and glories. But she has also unleashed her fair share of fury. Over its seventy-five years, Philmont has witnessed some dramatic natural disasters, and a few traumatic man-caused incidents. These were some of the events.

The Flood of 1965. The legendary Joe Davis started his decade-long tenure as camping director during a rain-drenched crisis. He arrived in May 1965, a late appointment following the unexpected death of his predecessor, Skipper Juncker. The rookie was greeted by heavy mid-day spring rains that saturated the ground. Davis headed up a staff of 500 and expected a record 15,000 Scouts to hike Philmont trails over the summer. June 18 was scheduled as "scatter" day, when staffers and equipment headed for the first time to the twenty-two backcountry camps. As the crews headed out mid-morning, big, black thunderclouds gathered. By noon, the deluge had started, and sheets of water continued to fall for the next four hours. A normal full year's worth of precipitation—fourteen inches—dropped in one afternoon. Only a few of the staff members made it to their assigned camps, and many were stranded. Damage was extensive: bridges were blown out, the water main to headquarters failed, the phones were knocked out, and the raging waters wreaked havoc on the trail system. About 400 Scouts were sched-

One rescue procedure during the 1965 operation involved some Philmont higher-ups, including Bill Littrell (in the cowboy hat) and Ray Bryan (on the far side of the creek).

uled to open Philmont's 1965 season. They were located while en route, and turned back. Davis, with support from Jack Rhea, set an ambitious goal to have the post-flood opening delayed by only one week. With high spirits, groups of ten rangers attacked the trail rebuilding. The Maintenance Department rebuilt a temporary water system. Trek itineraries were re-jiggered around damaged areas. Bridges were repaired. And after a week, campers began to arrive, and staff members, upon hearing

The Flood of 1965 took out bridges, trails, roads, and Philmont's water system.

Waters rage down the Rayado River during the June 18, 1965 flood, when fourteen inches of rain fell in one afternoon.

Davis announce the reopening, broke out in song: "It Ain't Gonna Rain No More." Philmont had survived the Flood of 1965 (which had ravaged communities from Denver to far south in New Mexico), with no loss of life, and only a small compromise to its schedule and program.

The Ponil Complex Fire, 2002. The largest conflagration in Philmont history came after several years of extreme drought and one of the lightest winters of snowpack ever in northern New Mexico. Four lightning-caused wildfires came together on June 2, and over the next fifteen days, burned 92,000 acres—more than 140 square miles—on Philmont and four of its neighbors. About a third of the burn zone, 28,000 acres, was Philmont's north country, though the eastern flank of Baldy Peak was spared. Other parcels hit included Valle Vidal, 25,000 acres; Ted Turner's Vermejo Park, 20,000 acres; the UU Bar Ranch, 15,000 acres; and the Barker Wildlife Area, 4,000 acres. The impact of the devastation was huge, both ecologically and for Philmont, operationally. The loss of trees and vegetation aided erosion and created mudflows. Native trout in Ponil Creek died from ash and debris. Due to the risk of flash flooding, Philmont closed its north country for the 2002 summer. Later, the ranch worked with federal and state agencies to restore what acreage it could by building dams, laying down straw, and seeding to create new ground cover.

The Ponil fire of 2002 jumped some sections in the canyons.

A flyover shows the extent of destruction of the Ponil Complex Fire of 2002.

The Ponil Complex Fire of 2002 burned about 28,000 acres of Philmont's north Ponil country, and 92,000 acres in all.

The crash of *Liberator 41-1133.* Seven Army Air Force flyers died on April 22, 1942, when their B-24 bomber crashed into Trail Peak, 10,242 feet high on Philmont. The crew had flown the four-engine plane on a training flight from Albuquerque to Kansas City on the morning of that fateful day, and was returning that night to the point of origin, Kirtland Field. Once back into New Mexico airspace, they ran into horrendous weather, and one of the four engines failed. Over Las Vegas, the bomber was steered back to the north, looking for a route around the massive storm system. It would not be found. All seven crewmembers died immediately upon impact on the southwest side of Trail Peak. William F. Cass, a Philmont staff veteran and author of *The Last Flight of Liberator 41-1133,* makes a compelling case in his book that the craft was caught in a downburst, where cold air rushes downward at a rate of several thousand feet per second. For several reasons, the crash stands out as unique from among the 490 stateside military plane crashes during World War II. With a steady stream of trekking Scouts each summer, the wreckage is the most visited aviation crash site in the world. Also of note, Chope Phillips, then twenty-four years old and using his estimable knowl-

edge of the Philmont terrain, guided the rescue party to the crash site, found by air after ten days of searching. One of the *41-1133* pilots, Lt. Roland Jeffries, was an Eagle Scout and introduced to aviation through Scouting in his hometown of Kansas City. Jeffries alone has a memorial plaque atop Trail Peak.

Forest fire, 1956: Spring and early summer typically constitute fire season, not only at Philmont, but also in most mountains of the West. On one day in May 1956, Director of Camping Jack Rhea was driving back to the ranch from Raton, enjoying the views of the western horizon. But he spotted a plume of smoke, its shape and color indicating a forest fire, near Philmont's southern border, Rayado country. According to Rhea's account, the next three weeks involved a massive effort—including hundreds of volunteering neighbors—to save Philmont. The fire was located on a ridge to the south of Rayado Canyon, and firefighters sought to prevent it from jumping the canyon and burning much of Philmont's scenic south country. The help Philmont received was wholly appreciated, and indicative of the local goodwill the Scouters had earned, Rhea said. "Their devotion to Philmont and determination to save it was a real credit to those who, through the years, had built a fine relationship with people on ranches and in communities nearby." A fire near Philmont's south border in June 2013 was eerily similar to the 1956 event.

The Fire of 1998. A lightning strike sparked a fire that burned about 4,300 acres, some on Philmont's north country, near the Dan Beard camp. It also burned acreage on the UU Bar Ranch and in the Carson National Forest.

Tornado, 1960. A tent city at Camping Headquarters took the brunt of a sudden windstorm that hit on June 20, 1960. Vince Matthews was a Scout on the scene. "Larry Gibbs and I were

Scouts pick up the pieces of a tent city at Camping HQ after a tornado touched down on June 20, 1960.

The skies over Philmont remained ominous after the 1960 tornado touched down.

the first out of the dining hall that evening. As we reached the quadrangle, the wind increased tremendously and Larry said he had to go inside because of the dust in his contacts. We ducked into an office in the quad. The wind and dust increased tremendously and then died abruptly. I went out and saw the tent city flattened and swept clean. The tornado was moving toward the Tooth of Time Ridge. It traveled from Ranger City across the flats to the ridge. The ridge forced it upward and as it lifted above the ridge it dropped its swirling load of tents, sleeping bags, and clothes on the far side of the ridge. The funnel dropped its payload, then continued up into the clouds and disappeared."

Airplane crash at Beaubien, 1953. Philmont's witness to a second aircraft disaster is far less known than the Trail Peak tragedy. Late in the summer, a single-engine plane was heard buzzing up Bonito

Canyon. The pilot tried to circle Lookout Meadow, but at an altitude of about seventy-five feet, his engine failed and the plane fell to earth. The Beaubien staff had been at breakfast, and reached the airplane in moments. The pilot was alive, but seriously injured with two broken legs, a broken arm, several broken ribs, and multiple lacerations. First aid was administered and the Philmont ambulance arrived within an hour to take the pilot to Raton. Ironically, the staff had earlier that summer determined that the meadows could be a landing site for many airplanes, and thus created the "Beaubien Air Force," replete with throw gliders, rubber band-powered gliders, and one gas engine model plane.

FAMOUS VISITORS

Philmont was visited by a host of the famous and notable

Over the years, Philmont has seen some notable people visit its mountains and participate in its programs.

Ansel Adams. The famed landscape photographer Ansel Adams came to Philmont with his cameras in 1962. His New Mexico-shot "Moonrise Over Hernandez" may be the iconic Adams photograph, but his work at Philmont, such as "Thunderstorm Over the Great Plains" and "Thunderhead Over Rayado Canyon" share similar lighting and drama.

Will Rogers. One of the best-known celebrities in the 1920s and 1930s, Will Rogers was a guest of Waite Phillips at Philmont during the final travels of his life. Rogers, a humorist, vaudeville and movie actor, and social commentator, landed at Philmont on July 26, 1935, with famed aviator Wiley Post. Rogers, who typed his newspaper columns while flying shotgun, headed with Post to Bellingham, Washington, where Post's plane was fitted with floats for water landings. The entire nation mourned when Rogers and Post died in a plane crash in Alaska on August 15, 1935, three weeks after the

Philmont touchdown. The crash was blamed on the incorrectly sized floats that made the plane front-heavy.

Donald Rumsfeld. Twice the nation's Secretary of Defense and chief of staff to President Ronald Reagan, Donald Rumsfeld worked at Philmont in 1949.

Norman Rockwell. America's painter, Norman Rockwell, visited Philmont in 1953 on his return from a National Scout Jamboree in California. What resulted was a classic Rockwell, "High Adventure," depicting enthusiastic Scouts and the Tooth of Time in the background. Early in his career, Rockwell worked as the art director for *Boys' Life*.

Jim Whittaker. The keynote speaker at the opening staff banquet in 2002 was Jim Whittaker, the first American climber to summit Mt. Everest.

Charles Dawes. Charles Dawes, vice president of the United States under President Calvin Coolidge from 1925 to 1929, visited Philmont as a guest

Vice President Charles Dawes was a guest of Waite Phillips at the Rayado Lodge.

Pilot Wiley Post, left, and humorist Will Rogers, right, were guests of Waite Phillips and grandson Phillips Breckinridge.

World-class climber and guide Wally Berg, a Philmont staff alumnus, delivered the keynote speech at the 2012 All Staff Gathering.

of Waite Phillips in July 1927, just as the Villa Philmonte was open, and again in the summer of 1928. Dawes had won the Nobel Peace Prize in 1925 for formulating the Germany reparations plan after World War I. From accounts of his visit, Dawes was known as a colorful and opinionated character. Dawes and his party enjoyed the 1927 visit so much, they returned in 1928.

Ben Ames Williams. Prolific novelist Ben Ames Williams was part of the Dawes visits, which included time at the Rayado Lodge (Fish Camp). His best-known novel, *Leave Her to Heaven*, uses Philmont as its backdrop. The book was made into a movie; producers scouted Philmont as a location before deciding to shoot it in Hollywood. The movie, which starred actress Gene Tierney, has been called a masterpiece. Also with Dawes and Williams were novelist Kenneth Roberts and *Chicago Tribune* cartoonist John McCutcheon.

Steve Fossett. World-record-setting flyer Steve Fossett served as a Philmont ranger in 1961. Fossett

died in a plane crash in 2007, but not before setting records for long balloon and aircraft flights.

William Sessions. William Sessions, then director of the Federal Bureau of Investigation, trekked Philmont in 1989 with his son. He had been on a trek as a youth, and on both expeditions, he climbed Old Baldy Mountain. That son, Pete, went on to become a U.S. congressman from Texas.

Wally Berg. For three summers from 1971 to 1973, climber Wally Berg guided as a ranger at Philmont. Today, Berg boasts more than forty-five ascents of the Seven Summits, the highest peaks of Earth's continents. Of those ascents, four were on Mt. Everest. Berg operates Berg Adventures International, one of the preeminent high-peak guiding services in the world. He spoke at the 2012 staff opening program and was given standing ovations and Philmont's Distinguished Staff Alumni Award.

Marlin Perkins. In 1964, Marlin Perkins filmed an episode of Mutual of Omaha's *Wild Kingdom* at Philmont. The program was one of the most popular on television at that time.

Marion Claussen. A couple of higher-ups in federal land management have visited Philmont and came away impressed. Marion Claussen, director of the Bureau of Land Management in the early 1950s and a renowned forester, termed Philmont as "an intensively managed wilderness." U.S. Secretary of the Interior Manuel Lujan visited Philmont in 1992 and was likewise favorably impressed. Lujan had been a longtime U.S. representative from the district that includes northern New Mexico.

GOING COED

Female Explorers become part of the Philmont experience

There were a few bumps in the road before young women were fully integrated into the Philmont program.

The Boy Scouts of America first opened its Explorer programs to girls in 1972. At Philmont, Camping

Director Joe Davis wasted no time in jumping on this bandwagon. He hired two young women, both sisters of existing Philmont staff members, as the first-ever female rangers.

The chosen pioneers were Kathy Leach, at the time a recent college graduate, and Nancy Wells, a wildlife biology major from Montana. The rangers, who gently protested when referred to as "rangerettes," first guided a group of five girl Explorers from Dallas. At the end of the summer, by all accounts, Leach and Wells had removed any doubts about their capabilities as full-fledged rangers. In fact, the next summer Leach earned the job of assistant chief ranger, and she led the first Kit Carson Women program.

Although it took a while for female rangers to be fully accepted in the formerly all-male domain, by 2013, thirty-four female rangers of about 250 were on staff. Christine Salisbury served as chief ranger

A 2009 girls Explorer group is all smiles on the trail to Baldy Mountain. (Photo courtesy of Philmont News and Photo Services)

The first female rangers at Philmont, left, Kathy Leach, and right, Nancy Wells, earned praise for performance in the ground-breaking summer of 1972. (Courtesy of the Philmont Museum archives)

for Philmont's seventy-fifth year, and Bridget Hogan was one of her four associate chief rangers.

TRAINING CENTER

Key component of adult leadership took time to develop

According to the wishes of Waite Phillips, one of Philmont Scout Ranch's three missions was for it to serve as a mecca for adult leadership training in the Boy Scouting program. The other two, of course, were to provide outdoor opportunities for boys, and to remain a working cattle ranch.

That leadership training goal took the better part of a decade after the second Phillips donation to come to full fruition. Once the Philmont Training Center (known for some time as the Volunteer Training

Center) formally got off the ground in 1951, it succeeded handsomely in fulfilling that mission.

The first adult training at Philmont took place in the fall of 1943, a course for about fifty Scouters on finance. The course, soon tabbed the "Diamond Hitch," an efficient and essential knot used in burro packing, was held annually. After World War II, the Diamond Hitch finance course grew in popularity.

In 1948, Philmont hosted one of the first two Woodbadge courses in the United States. Woodbadge was created in England by Lord Baden-Powell, the founder of the Boy Scout movement. In Woodbadge, adult leaders gained outdoor and leadership skills through a "learn by doing" method. For a week in early October, thirty-five men camped at Cimarroncito. An earlier U.S. Woodbadge had been held in August at Schiff Scout Reservation in New Jersey.

Though the Training Center is headquartered on the grounds of the Villa Philmonte, adult leaders, like these in 2010, enjoy learning free of walls.

a major expansion of the training area was planned and approved. A vital component was the creation of a "tent city" east of the Villa. Canvas walled tents, seven by nine feet in size, were erected on solid wooden platforms and equipped with cots and mattresses. A shower/laundry building was constructed. The tent city had the capability of housing one hundred participants and family members.

Participants in a 1950s session at the Volunteer Training Center pose at the Villa.

In 1949, the Woodbadge program was relocated to the Zastrow camp, west of Rayado, where a lodge was constructed. Since 1973, Woodbadge sessions have been run by local councils utilizing Philmont facilities.

Meanwhile, the increasing popularity of the traditional adult training programs in the late 1940s exposed the need for additional facilities on the grounds of Villa Philmonte, which functioned imperfectly as a venue for the courses. In 1950,

From the get-go, the intention was for the Training Center to be utilized by the adult leaders, but also by their families—wives and children were most decidedly welcome. While the male leader was busy in conferences, the children were organized into groups by age and gender, with daily programs and activities. Mothers and wives were free to attend training sessions, help with the children's programs, tour the area, or participate in craft programs.

Philmont's new training offerings were an immediate success. In 1952, the program enrolled about 800 Scouters over eighteen courses. An auditorium-dining room complex was constructed south of the Villa. A second tent city, playgrounds, a pony ring, a craft lodge, and game areas were soon added. A four-classroom building was built in 1954, and three new duplexes provided for staff housing.

By the late 1950s, attendance at the Training Center grew to nearly 4,000, and since that time, the facility has steadily served about 5,000 Scout leaders and family members each summer. The Philmont Training Center continues to make good on the benevolent vision of Waite Phillips.

CHAPTER 5
PHILMONT TODAY

THE TREK

Young hikers find challenge, education, fun on Philmont trails

For better than fifty years, Philmont's core program has involved crews of Boy Scouts and Explorers traveling on foot for eleven days between backcountry camps. It's the trek—designed to test fitness, build character and self-confidence, emphasize teamwork, teach wilderness skills, and, darn it, just have some fun in the great outdoors.

What does today's standard trek look like?

For the 2013 summer, the Scout Ranch offered thirty-five distinct pre-planned itineraries, rang-

A red-shirted ranger looks over a trek route with two Scout leaders.

ing from fifty-seven to 104 miles in length. Each itinerary has stops at up to ten backcountry camps, some staffed and with facilities, some not. A few itineraries have two consecutive overnights at the larger camps: Beaubien, Cimarroncito, Ewells Park, Miranda, Baldy Town, Black Horse, Ute Meadows, Maxwell, and Copper Park.

As Scouting crews plan their New Mexico expedition, they select five choices out of Philmont's annual Itinerary Guide. Factors they consider include length, terrain, degree of difficulty, and activities and programs offered in the camps. Itineraries are graded from "challenging" to "rugged" to "strenuous" to "super strenuous."

A crew leader and advisors from South Carolina check into the Philmont Welcome Center.

A backpack-laden crew hikes through a meadow outside Miranda, and under Baldy.

Philmont stresses that the itinerary be selected by the Scouts who will be hiking it, not adult leaders, and encourages a democratic selection process. Once a crew makes its five top choices, they are submitted via Internet in March before their trek that summer (seventeen months earlier, they would have registered and been picked lottery fashion for a trek spot). Philmont draws itineraries, also by lottery, that April, so as to prevent logistical logjams.

And the trip to Philmont is made. A crew is required to have from two to four adult advisors and a majority of youth participants. Designating a youth crew leader is strongly advised. Crews get to Cimarron by all travel means—bus, train, air, and convoy. They arrive at Philmont between 8 and 11 a.m. on their scheduled day. The expedition begins with lunch at the Camping Headquarters Dining Hall. That afternoon, participants meet their assigned staff ranger, undergo a medical recheck, get assigned to sleeping quarters in the Trailbound Tent City, pick up food and trail equipment, tour the HQ facilities and the Villa Philmonte if time allows, and importantly, go through a "shakedown" where rangers help the would-be hikers lighten their loads to bare essentials. That night, the new crews hear *The Philmont*

A variety of terrain, including some wet ones, challenge Scouts out on the trail.

Story, a lively pageant that tells the rich history of the Cimarron area and Philmont.

After breakfast at the Dining Hall on Day 2, a bus picks up the crew at the Martin Welcome Center and transports them to a location near the first camp. Let's say the crew has been given Itinerary No. 1, 2013. The bus will take them to a drop-off point east of Cathedral Rock, the outcropping that

Burros add some four-legged personality and interaction to most treks.

Challenge courses at the Uracca and Head of Dean camps foster teamwork to overcome obstacles.

overlooks Cimarroncito Reservoir. After a short hike to the Cathedral Rock trail camp, the crew's ranger will work with Scouts on hiking tips, camping skills, map and compass, safety and first aid, fire building and cooking, water and sanitation, the Wilderness Pledge, and conservation and low-impact practices, as well as safe bear, mountain lion, and wilderness practices.

Day 3 will see the crew head out and hike the first leg of their trek, along with their ranger. They will set out via Window Rock and Hidden Valley for the Cimarroncito camp, gaining about 500 feet of elevation. They will also enjoy their first crack at one of the forty interesting, educational, and fun programs. At 'Cito, they can climb rocks and boulders, then rappel back down. On the morning of Day 4, the ranger will head back to HQ and leave the crew to its own devices, assured the group can handle the rigors of the trek. This day's hike heads west and uphill through aspen groves to Cyphers Mine. It is the first of two days of some serious climbing, though Scouts coming from hot-weather climes enjoy the cool mountain air. Activities include gold panning, blacksmithing, and the notorious evening "stomp," some good-time mining music. The strenuous fifth-day leg climbs to Mt. Phillips Camp, at 11,650 feet of elevation the ranch's highest camp, with no water or staff. It's on the eastern flank of its namesake. No fun and games here, as tuckered crew members have just climbed 2,290 vertical feet over about eight miles, all with full packs on their backs.

Twenty miles down, about thirty-seven to go, but most are downhill, as Camping HQ sits nearly a vertical mile below Mt. Phillips. The Day 6 hike will start by knocking off the peak's summit, an elevation of 11,736 feet. After enjoying expansive views, including New Mexico-high-point Wheeler Peak to the west and Baldy to the north, the crew will head down into the Rayado Creek drainage. Just off the peak is Clear Creek Camp, where a fur-trapping outpost has been re-created, the Rocky Mountain Fur Company. The program offers black-

Shooting programs at six backcountry camps add a kick to the trek. Firearms include black powder rifles, lever action rifles, 12-gauge shotguns, and 30.06 rifles.

From Basecamp, which way to go? With about ninety camps in the backcountry, hiking crews have plenty of options, with thirty-five itineraries offered in 2013.

Hanging a bear bag, containing all of the food and anything that might attract a bruin into camp, is a time-honored and daily Philmont exercise.

Ah, nothing like getting a load off the back and feet en route to the next night's camp!

A crew descends Old Baldy Mountain, the summit of the Scout Ranch.

Rayado program participants get high-fives all around from rangers after completing the grueling twenty-day program, which stresses leadership and advanced outdoor skills.

powder shooting and a trapping demonstration. The hike continues down to the Comanche Creek trail camp.

The trek's Day 7 points downstream to Apache Springs, an elevation of 9,360 feet. But before there, the crew will stop to perform conservation work near Buck Creek. Into Apache Springs, with

tepees set up in a peaceful meadow, Scouts will learn of Jicarilla Apache ways. Activities include a sweat lodge and a 3-D archery range. The itinerary dictates a welcome second night here. The Day 9 leg goes to Waite Phillips's favorite spot on Philmont, Fish Camp. Here, Urraca Ranch owner George Webster erected a cabin in 1908, which Phillips later lavished with a rustic millionaire's

After the trek, well-worn boots earn their place of honor on the Philmont gate.

touch. True to its name, the program here is about fly-tying and fishing, and the Phillips legacy.

A long, downhill hike proceeds on Day 10 past Lookout, Crater, and Rayado peaks, and through the Notch, to Abreu Camp, which honors the Mexican heritage of the Philmont area. Here, Scouts will be treated to a Mexican dinner, a cantina, and showers. They will be introduced to search and rescue and wilderness medicine. The final day of full hiking points to the Stockade Ridge trail camp, in the southern shadow of the Tooth of Time.

On Day 12 of 12, Scouts will hike up Philmont's iconic landmark, the Tooth, then an easy down-hill into Camping HQ. The trek culminates in the climactic Awards Campfire, a night in the

Homebound Tent City, a Day 13 breakfast, and a happy, more mature bunch of youth headed home. A "WE ALL MADE IT!" plaque symbolizes the crew's collective achievement.

BACKCOUNTRY

Camps offer diversity of terrain, program, experiences

Waite Phillips entertained a grand vision for his grand mountain ranch. Donated to the Boy Scouts of America, it would become "a university of the out-of-doors"—Waite's words—that would help teen-aged boys learn of wilderness ways and gain character, much as he had seen occur with his son and nephews.

But any university needs classrooms, even ones in the out-of-doors. At Philmont, those classrooms are found at the thirty-four staffed backcountry camps scattered across the ranch's 214 square miles. And at some fifty-plus other rustic trail camps where young hikers learn not only about camping, cooking, and conservation, but also about self-reliance, teamwork, and newfound maturity.

Through its three-quarters of a century of ownership, the Boy Scouts organization has taken the wondrous terrain it was bequeathed—ranging from foothills rangeland to piñon-covered canyonlands to majestic aspen-covered peaks—and overlaid it with a system of camps, then developed programs of history, skill, fun, and challenge.

Put together this combination—the mountainous "God's Country," the rustic backcountry camps, the jovial staff interpreters, and the inventive programs that educate, enrich, and entertain—and we have the Philmont Experience.

The camps and the programs they host are essential pieces of that. Longtime Philmont staff member and camp director Rock Rohrbacher has authored seven editions over fifteen years of the delightful book *Philmanac*, a compendium of all things Philmont: facts, historical lists, trivia, photos, a catalog of latrine styles, patches, maps... and an exhaustively complete description of the ranch's backcountry camps. Excerpted from Rohrbacher's compilation, here are brief summaries of twenty interesting staffed backcountry camps, by region.

SOUTHEAST

New Abreu. Named for a Rayado-area pioneer family, this camp was built in the mid-1960s, and in the last twenty-five years has been used as an interpretive camp to recreate a Hispanic-American homestead, similar to what Petra and Jesus Abreu might have left behind around the time New Mexico became a state in 1912. Scouts are treated

Scouts hanging out at the New Abreu cantina.

Making adobe bricks is a dirty business.

Time through Stonewall Pass. The staffed camp is Philmont's newest, having originated in 2005. Scouts gain skills in search and rescue while camping here.

here to a Mexican dinner, a cantina (nothing stronger than root beer), and showers. New Abreu replaced Old Abreu, which was overused, then largely washed out in the Flood of 1965.

Carson Meadows. This camp offers fifteen campsites and a breathtaking view of the Tooth of

Cimarroncito. One of the larger staffed camps on Philmont, Cimarroncito ("little wild boy") served for years as base camp for the ranch's central country. Waite Phillips's hunting lodge is found here. The mini-city stretches for nearly a mile in an expansive valley at 8,140 feet, and boasts a wide range of facilities, including an indoor climbing

Rescue techniques are taught at Carson Meadows.

Top: A Scout scales a wall at Cimarroncito.

Above: Proper rope technique is essential to safety on the rocks.

wall, three chapels, and volleyball courts. 'Cito's primary program consists of rock climbing and rappelling. Twenty-three totem poles add an interesting attraction at the camp. Most were carved between 1948 and 1956 by crews on the Wagon Train program, which typically camped here for four days.

The activity turns vertical at Miners Park.

Urraca. This seventeen-site camp has seen a variety of programs over the years, including astronomy, rock climbing, bow hunting, survival, plants and dyes, and search and rescue. Today, the program is the Urraca Challenge, one of two obstacle courses at Philmont that Scouts negotiate. It emphasizes problem solving, fitness, and teamwork. Urraca is near Inspiration Point, which boasts views worthy of its name.

Miners Park. Known as "rock climbing paradise," the park is situated in a meadow near the Tooth of Time where miners and their families used to gather. Climbing takes place on a unique two-rock formation called Betty's Bra, about a mile off from the meadow.

An Explorer finds the heights of the COPE (Challenging Outdoor Personal Experience) course near Rocky Mountain Scout Camp.

Scouts relax on the Fish Camp porch, just like Waite Phillips and some of his famous friends did.

At Fish Camp, young fishermen tie their own flies.

SOUTHWEST

Fish Camp. George Webster, the owner of the land prior to Waite Phillips, first built a cabin here at the confluence of the Rayado and Agua Fria creeks, at an elevation of 8,480 feet. The Webster cabin burned down shortly after Phillips bought it, and the millionaire oilman didn't cut corners when he built lodges at this special location. His Rayado Lodge was perhaps Phillips's favorite place on the ranch, and he brought many guests and family to

Bow and arrows fly at Apache Springs.

enjoy the place. He wanted the area preserved as wilderness, therefore no road was built; visitors arrived by horseback. The Flood of 1965 hit Fish Camp hard, turning a grassy meadow into a debris field and washing out the trail along the Rayado River. Today, Fish Camp has ten campsites, and naturally, the program involves fly-tying and fishing. Camp staff dress as 1920s-era guides and teach Scouts how to catch the five varieties of trout that inhabit the streams.

Apache Springs. This camp lies among pristine terrain at the far southwestern corner of the ranch, high up at 9,360 feet. It was established in 1965 to absorb some of the traffic from flooded-out Fish Camp. For the last forty years, the program has highlighted the life and times of the Jicarilla Apache who lived, and thrived, in the region in the early 1700s. Authentic teepees occupy an aspen-ringed park, and a sweat lodge introduces visiting Scouts to tribal traditions. They enjoy archery, as well.

Teepees create a visual exclamation point in Apache Springs meadow.

Top: It's high-country heaven at the Beaubien camp.

Above: Anybody up for a horseback ride in the mountains?

Beaubien. Nestled among the Bonito, Black Mountain, and Trail peaks, Beaubien serves as the central hub for the south country, boasting the largest number of campsites—thirty-four—and crew loads. It's the largest staffed camp on Philmont. The activities theme centers on Western lore, with horse riding, branding, a chuckwagon dinner, and an evening campfire. A two-night stopover here is on several itineraries, and Scouts often partake

The lassos fly at the roping practice station.

Backcountry staff mines hard-rock history at Cyphers.

Scouts go where the sun doesn't shine to learn about mining.

of side-hikes up to the bomber wreckage on Trail Peak. Beaubien is named for Charles Beaubien, the Canadian-born fur trapper who was the original recipient of the largest land grant in U.S. history, together with Guadalupe Miranda.

Cyphers Mine. Charlie Cypher operated a mine here and lived in a cabin in the Cimarroncito mining district, up until Waite Phillips paid him to leave in the 1920s. Today, Charlie's Cabin contains artifacts and tools from the old mining days, and is the scene for the evening music "stomps." A new cabin/mining office was built in 2002, and Scouts here participate in blacksmithing, gold mining, and panning. Cyphers features wood-stoked hot showers.

It's Philmont's version of the mall—the commissary at Phillips Junction.

Phillips Junction. Technically not a camp, "PJ" might best be considered a pit stop. Within hiking distance of six staffed southwest country camps, PJ serves as a commissary for food pickup (largest on the ranch) and as a trading post. The outpost lies due south of Bonito Peak and east of Trail Peak, at 8,880 feet. After a stop here, crews continue to overnight camps at Apache Springs, Beaubien, Black Mountain, Clear Creek, Crooked Creek, or Fish Camp.

NORTHEAST

Ponil. For the three years of its operation, the Philturn Rockymountain Scoutcamp was head-

quartered here. The site was originally known as Five Points, where a handful of canyons converged. About a dozen cabins have been built at Ponil over the years, the most of any Philmont camp. Only through concentrated effort were the structures spared from the Ponil Complex Fire of 2002. The camp's program, as it has been since the Philturn days, consists of horseback riding and Western lore. And a chuckwagon supper, pancake breakfast, and

Hoe-downs at Ponil entertain Scouts after a tough hike.

Ponil was the original camp as Philturn Rockymountain Scoutcamp.

The Western ways of life, including shooting, are learned by doing.

A program counselor provides the history of an Anasazi petroglyph.

campfire shows have been added over the summers. Ponil get its name from a plant, the Apache plume, which has five points.

Indian Writings. Located in North Ponil Canyon, a ridge across from Ponil camp, Indian Writings showcases petroglyphs left by the Anasazis prior to the fourteenth century. The camp was one of the first to be used at Philturn in 1939, and was the target of the fabled Philturn Archaeological Expedition in 1941. A six-Scout crew from New Haven, Connecticut, was trained in archaeological methods by the staff at Yale's Peabody Museum, and then spent a month cataloging ancient Indian artifacts they uncovered at Indian Writings. At 6,660 feet, the camp is one of lowest on the ranch.

Dan Beard. The northernmost camp within Philmont boundaries, this camp is known for its challenge course, rock climbing, low-impact camping education, and as a staging area for crews heading into the Valle Vidal. The camp was not staffed for twenty years until 1989, when Philmont gained permission to hike and camp in the national forest land of the Valle Vidal. "Uncle Dan" Beard was a legendary Scouting pioneer from Ohio.

Dean Cow. Climbing here is on sandstone, unlike the hard-rock venues at more southern climbing camps. Crews are advised to get on the trails into Dean Cow early in the day, and the canyons are typically hot and dry by afternoon. Dean Cow is on Philmont's eastern border in cattle country, and Bob Dean was a one-time cattle foreman in these parts.

Climbing at Dean Cow is on gritty sandstone rock.

Opposite page: Teammates give a boost on the COPE course at Dan Beard.

NORTHWEST

Miranda. A mountain man rendezvous interpretive program highlights a visit to this Baldy region camp, created in the mid-1960s after Philmont gained the Clapp acreage. Crews shoot black powder rifles, throw tomahawks, and learn about the mountain men of the 1830s and their gatherings. Miranda's eighteen campsites sit in an aspen-surrounded meadow at 8,960 feet and it is known as one of Philmont's most beautiful locations.

Baldy Camp. Once a thriving community with over twenty buildings and a population of 1,000, Baldy Town was the center of prosperous but sporadic mining activity from 1868 to 1940. The Aztec, with seven levels of tunnels, was the largest of the mines on the southeast flank of Baldy Mountain. Building

Top: Miranda's idyllic cabin is an oasis on the mountain.

Above: Scouts don't want to mess around with a tough Miranda mountain man.

Is there any gold left in tham thar Baldy hills?

A Scout reaches new heights on a Pueblano spar pole.

foundations and the rubble of the Aztec Mill, destroyed by fire in 1923, remain at the camp. Twelve campsites are scattered among aspen trees at 9,920 feet. The camp commissary is at the site of the old town school.

Pueblano. The "little village" camp was on the western edge of Philmont until the Clapp donation added the Baldy country to the ranch. Pueblano reopened as a staffed camp in 1977, with the rich

Logging is a heavy occupation, Scouts find.

legacy of timbering in the area as its program. Crewmembers climb spar poles with the help of the men of the Continental Tie & Lumber Co., which worked in the Ponil canyons from 1907 to 1930. Pueblano sits midway on the Miranda-Ponil burro-packing route.

French Henry. Scouts get a look into Level 2 of the Aztec Mine by hiking from Baldy Camp over Aztec Ridge to French Henry and entering a portal. They also pan for gold in South Ponil Creek, tour the mining museum in a cabin, and watch a black-smithing demonstration. The camp is named for Henri Buruel, who bought the mining rights from Lucien Maxwell in the 1860s. His French Henry mine sunk its shaft sixty feet vertically into the rock, but Buruel had no mill to process his ore, and Maxwell's Aztec Mill over the hill was busy with its own mine product. No camping facilities are found at French Henry, so crews head on to neighboring

Hard-rock mining in French Henry was, well, hard.

outposts, such as Miranda, Baldy Camp, Ewells Park, or Upper Greenwood.

VALLE VIDAL

Ring Place. Crews get a glimpse of frontier ranching life here, where Tim Ring, a one-armed Civil War veteran, homesteaded with his wife and seven daughters. Ring purchased 320 acres from the Maxwell Land Grant Company in 1890 for $960. He built a fifteen-room homestead. In modern times it has remained boarded up, though that has served as no deterrent

Ring Place was the scenic homestead of a one-armed Civil War veteran and his family.

Backcountry staff erect the yurt at Whiteman Vega for the summer.

At Whiteman Vega, Scouts get around on two wheels.

to rats and vermin. With no established trails in the Valle Vidal, Philmont hikers have to use map and compass. They overnight at the McCrystal Creek campground, across the road from the Ring Place.

Whiteman Vega. Southeast of Ash Mountain and Little Costilla peak in the Carson National Forest, the camp hosts Philmont's mountain biking and "bikathon" program. The latter is similar to the

Olympics' biathlon, except Scouts bicycle instead of ski and use air rifles when they stop at points to shoot at targets. Philmont put in a Mongolian-style yurt here as a permanent staff cabin. Wildlife, especially elk, abounds in this part of the Valle Vidal.

THE STAFF

All-important facilitators help make experience special

Continuing with Waite Phillips's "university of the out-of-doors" metaphor, where the backcountry camps are the classrooms, it follows that Philmont's staff are the professors.

Through the decades, Philmont can boast of having thousands of fantastic professors, the staff members who have helped make the Philmont experience

more than just a mere campout, and no less than a life-affecting journey.

Indeed, current program director Mark Anderson identifies the Scout Ranch's staff as one of the five pillars of the Philmont brand. (The other four: Philmont's "unique pile of rocks," its rich history, the Phillips legacy, and common memories made.) Nearly without exception, staff members, now and through the years, have been of exceptionally high caliber. That should come as no surprise, as the Boy Scout law calls on its members to exhibit the characteristics of being trustworthy, loyal, helpful, friendly, courteous, kind, obedient, cheerful, thrifty, brave, clean, and reverent. Most of the Philmont staff has come from the cream of the Boy Scouting crop.

Organization and quality manpower are required to keep the Philmont machine firing on all cylin-

Backcountry staff dress in period costume to create living history, and music is often part of the program, such as with this Crater Lake bluegrass troupe in 2009.

Philmont's summer seasons kick off each June with the All Staff Gathering.

Philmont staff members take pride in the department in which they serve, and group photos for the annual Yearbook are known to be a bit wild and crazy.

ders at a facility that hosts some 30,000 visitors a year. To do that, Philmont Scout Ranch employs eighty full-time permanent employees, but then bulks up for its prime time each summer by hiring 1,080 seasonal workers.

Perhaps the most important people on the Philmont staff are the rangers and the program counselors at staffed camps (who refer to their job title as simply "backcountry"). They are the ones on the front lines who deliver the person-to-person experiences. It is they who teach, advise, assure, and support the trekking youngsters and their adult advisors. The rangers make sure visiting Scout crews on the trail get off to a good start for the first days of the trek. The "backcountry" at the camps, which have either historical or activity themes, help educate, entertain, and befriend their visitors. With their interpretive skills, they bring history alive, and ensure that the Scouts learn new and sometimes risky activities in a safe manner.

Philmont has always asked its staffers to aspire to inspire.

Dave Bates, director of camping from 1987 to 1994, perfectly described the challenge for his staff members when he addressed them at the start of Philmont's fiftieth year, in 1988:

"Hopefully Philmont accomplishes its mission to provide outdoor adventures and activities that help young people grow in character, become better citizens, and become increasingly fit physically, emotionally, and spiritually. The example of each and every staff member has a tremendous impact on campers and participants.

"Before a trek, participants are eager for adventure, excitement, and fun. Many of them are a bit apprehensive about their forthcoming adventure that will probably include some unexpected events. Some participants are boisterous, irreverent, or rambunctious; others are unsure of themselves and tend to be withdrawn. Some are cocky,

some are argumentative, some are whiny, and most are inquisitive.

"What characterizes young people as they conclude their trek? If we have been successful, they are more cooperative and more willing to pitch in to do whatever needs doing. They tend to be more patient with others; they have a better sense of group dynamics and they have a sense of camaraderie. Most will be exuberant and enthusiastic—they will have a sense of genuine accomplishment. We hope they are better motivated and willing to take more initiative. We want each one to be more confident, better able to deal with problems and better able to communicate with others. Certainly the parents and leaders of Philmont participants hope that the Philmont experience will achieve all this and more.

"It's up to each one of us to ask himself or herself, 'How can I (we) make this happen? How can I (we) help campers and participants grow? How can I (we) ensure that each and every one will have a lasting experience?' Let us set an example that will cause young people to think, 'I'd like to be like him' or 'I'd like to do what she does.' With high Philmont standards, we will impact the lives of 24,000 people for their lifetimes and beyond. The Philmont experience will last forever."

THE PHILMONT BOND

Staff Association provides vehicle for reuniting, service

Teamwork. Friendship. Camaraderie. Bonding.

Those are things that happen when you put a bunch of young, intelligent, energetic, and well-intentioned young adults on the same team. We're referring here to the Philmont staffs of the past seventy-five years.

Such mountain-made connections obviously don't vanish once a Philmont summer season ends. But for the first thirty-five years of the Scout Ranch, any

Philmont Staff Association members get together annually for a reunion trek on the ranch.

post-Philmont interaction between staff or ex-staff members happened simply by individual initiative or chance. That changed in 1973, when a former ranger, Ned Gold Jr., led an organizing committee that created the Philmont Staff Association. Its stated goal: To reunite those who worked on the ranch, and to provide a continuing interest in and support for the mission and programs of Philmont.

Today, the Philmont Staff Association numbers about 2,700 strong, and boasts a long list of projects and accomplishments in forty years of work.

Some of the PSA's undertakings have been ambitious, and highly beneficial to current staffers who have succeeded PSA's members. The organization raised more than $1 million for construction of the Silver Sage Staff Activity Center, which opened in 2008. In 1999, the PSA generated $300,000 in donations to build a new staff dining hall.

Other PSA service projects completed over the years have included ten cabin restorations at backcountry camps, Rayado scholarships, Baldy Town historical signs, and, after the 2002 Ponil Complex Fire, restocking native Rio Grande cutthroat trout in Ponil Creek.

The PSA is not a typical non-profit organization. Its funding comes almost wholly from the donations of its members, and not outside sources. In 1999, the PSA created its Annual Fund, with monies used to provide scholarships for summer staff, fund Philbreak, publish the PSA's award-winning magazine, *High Country*, and provide other general Philmont support. A typical Annual Fund goal is to raise $75,000.

For Philmont's seventy-fifth anniversary, the PSA set its sights Baldy Peak—high. It launched Campaign4Philmont, an effort to raise $1.4 million for four specific projects. They are: replacement of the advisors' meeting facility at Camping Headquarters; period-appropriate furnishings at backcountry camps; facility improvements at the Philmont Training Center, including improved handicap accessibility; and scholarship support for seasonal staff, to help retain the "best of the best."

PRESERVING HISTORY

Museums, library provide education center, look at Philmont

Ernest Thompson Seton never made it to Philmont, but that doesn't mean he didn't deserve a place here. The naturalist, artist, writer, and cofounder of the Boy Scouts of America was invited to the Scout Ranch by an early Philmont boss in 1946, and Seton had agreed to come. Sadly, before he made the trip from his Santa Fe home, Seton died that October at age eighty-six.

He left behind a voluminous collection of work: thousands of sketches of wild animals and birds, thousands of wildlife skins and pelts, hundreds of paintings, and a collection of Indian artifacts. And Seton owned what was believed to be the nation's largest library of natural history books, some 20,000 volumes.

Seton's widow Julia and a trusted friend from the Boy Scouts, Wes Klusman, had always thought Philmont might be a good landing spot for the Seton collection, if a proper setting existed. It took twenty-one years and the construction of a dedicated museum building for Seton's collection to find its way to the Scout Ranch. The Ernest Thompson Seton Memorial Library and Museum was dedicated on June 15, 1967.

Today, the facility serves as Philmont's education center, its history book, its conscience (by examining Philmont's mission and values), and a gateway to memories for those with a connection to the Scout Ranch.

The role of the renamed Philmont Museum and Seton Memorial Library changes with the seasons, according to Director Dave Werhane. "As staff arrive in May, we become the primary resource of historical knowledge. During the course of their jobs, most of our staff will be required to share the history of Philmont with our participants. One reason Waite Phillips believed this land to be spe-

The handsome stucco facility sits across the highway from Camping Headquarters.

cial was the diverse history which had transpired on it. He believed that the story of its people, from Native Americans to American heroes, such as Kit Carson, would help build character and inspire the youth of America."

Werhane notes that as the summer progresses, staff members continue to further their knowledge, and that visiting participants, from both the Camping and Training operations, discover that the museum/library is well heeled with artifacts and reading material to help quench the thirst to "know more about Philmont, this amazing place in our amazing history and this wondrous gift."

With autumn and winter come those seeking out their past, and the Philmont Museum steps up to

The museum and library was created in 1967, and a major expansion project is planned.

Museum Director Dave Werhane works with kids on a project. Behind him mounted on the wall is the pelt of Lobo.

Ernest Thompson Seton in his younger days.

help rekindle their memories of an adventure, an adventure that likely changed their lives. "Those visitors are easy to spot," said Werhane. "Before the door closes we are greeted with, 'I was here in...'" Then there is the spring and the museum shifts toward helping school groups, historic trail associations, and various other wandering history buffs. This is also when serious backcountry staff begin making contact, requesting detailed history for their upcoming summer jobs."

Werhane concludes: "All in all we see the full circle here; the day a young participant first learns about our amazing history, that young adult then coming back to work here and immersing themselves in our history, passing it on to all those they meet, and then finally coming back years later to use us as a guide to remember how it all started."

The museum, south of the Villa Philmonte and across the road from Camping Headquarters, was

The painting, *Triumph of the Wolves*, hangs in the library.

Seton's working sketch for his painting.

built with funds donated by Mr. and Mrs. L. O. Crosby, of Picayune, Mississippi. The handsome structure, which features Southwest adobe-style architecture, houses the library in its north wing a bookstore/gift shop in the center, and museum exhibit halls in the south wing.

While the first-rate exhibits help enrich the Philmont story and experience, the two main-stay attractions of the facility are found on the library walls. One is the pelt of Lobo, the massive alpha wolf that Seton trapped in far northeast New Mexico in the mid-1890s. The second is Seton's masterpiece of a painting, *Triumph of the Wolves*, picturing a handful of wolves with one gnawing on a human skull. In 1891, Seton had a painting, *The Sleeping Wolf*, selected by the Salon, the prestigious biennial art exhibit at the Louvre in Paris. Seton wanted to build

on this impressive success with an even larger, more impressive work. He painted *Triumph* in 1892. However, the Salon Jury rejected the piece; speculation centered on several reasons for this. Perhaps they disapproved of a message where nature had triumphed over man, perhaps the subject was unpalatable, or maybe it was just too unconventional.

On grounds outside of the museum are two additional attractions. A chiseled face peers out from

How cool is an operational (and free!) pinball machine in a museum exhibition? The pinball machine was designed by George Gomez, a Philmont staff alumnus.

a boulder placed along the entrance walkway. The stone face constitutes one of Philmont's biggest mysteries. Before being relocated to the museum to protect it from vandalism, the boulder sat on a piñon-covered hill on Philmont property several miles west of Cimarron. Some have called it the "Christ Face"; others said it was the likeness of outlaw Black Jack Ketchum, a lookout for his hideout. Museum visitors can also study a life-sized replica of the *Tyrannosaurus rex* track that was discovered in Philmont's North Ponil Canyon.

For its seventy-fifth anniversary, the Philmont Museum featured an exhibit, "The Gift of Inspiration," which showcased fourteen artists and creators who were positively affected by their Philmont experience as staff members. The artworks ranged from acrylic paintings to photography to a very popular working pinball machine. "The artists displayed could not have become the people they are today without their journey here at Philmont," the exhibit notes.

Cimarron sculptor Susan Norris has been commissioned for life-sized works of Ernest Thompson Seton with a Scout and of Lobo.

Some exciting additions loom on the museum's horizon. Philmont launched a capital campaign to raise $6 million to expand the facility. When complete, the expansion will increase the current facility by more than 7,500 square feet. The addition will more than double the gallery space, create much-needed archive storage, and construct a scholar room, reading room, artifact workshop, and large meeting room capable of seating more than sixty people for lectures, seminars, programs, workshops, and other museum events.

In 2013, Philmont commissioned two life-sized bronze sculptures: one of Lobo, and one of Ernest Thompson Seton and a Boy Scout. The creations by Cimarron artist/sculptor Susan Norris are to greet visitors along the walkway to the museum entrance.

The Villa Philmonte is under the auspices of the Museum Department, while the Kit Carson Museum has been hosting Scouts in Rayado since 1951.

Early on, Philmont officials realized the historical importance of the old Carson home, and its educational potential. In 1946, when the crumbling adobe structure had only three rooms left standing, Philmont held a picnic for family members of Rayado settlers, including members of the Abreu and Zastrow families. The old-timers, including Jesus Abreu's son Narciso, helped recreate the floor plan of the old Carson home for a planned reconstruction. That work started in 1949, on the centennial anniversary of Kit Carson moving his family from Taos to Rayado at the invitation of Lucien Maxwell.

The project was completed in 1951, successfully preserving as much historical authenticity as possible. The Kit Carson Museum is a classic New Mexican hacienda, a square building built around a courtyard. The walls were rebuilt with real adobe bricks made by the Philmont Service Corps. Ceilings are supported by pine log beams, or vigas. A torreon (lookout and bell tower) used to poke above the southwest corner, but was removed in the late 1970s.

Through the years, the Kit Carson Museum has displayed old wagons and stagecoaches, the likes of which would have been traveling the Santa Fe Trail. Fiery demonstrations have shown how blacksmiths kept the wagons on the trail. The home's rooms feature furnishings typical of the 1850s.

Lastly, in November 2013, Philmont took the storied Chase Ranch under its umbrella in a long-term lease agreement with a foundation set up by the late Gretchen Sammis. Plans include using the historic ranch house, a few miles up the Ponil road, as a museum to highlight the long Chase family era and the area's ranching life. The museum at the Chase will be Philmont's fourth facility.

THE BIG WOLF

Philmont preserves the story of Lobo, whose story changed America

Ernest Thompson Seton grew up with wolves on the Canadian frontier, and became an expert at trapping and hunting them. Thus, he was lured to the Currumpaw Valley in far northeastern New Mexico in 1893 by a $1,000 bounty put on the head of Lobo, a pack leader known as the King of Currumpaw. The wolves, having seen their food sources, such as the buffalo, eradicated by encroaching civilization, were preying on ranch livestock.

Lobo foiled all efforts at hunting or trapping him, including Seton's. The wily wolf would refuse to eat poisoned meat (and even defecated on one serving) and would cleverly disarm traps that were set. As the job stretched unsuccessfully from weeks to months, Seton hatched a new strategy, to trap Lobo's mate, Blanca, and use her as bait. Finally, she was caught, and Seton found her howling, with Lobo at her side. She was cruelly killed, with ropes pulled by horses breaking her neck.

In the following days, Lobo cried for his mate. Seton described it with "an unmistakable note of

Seton sketched his quarry in *A Royal Captive.*

sorrow in it. It was no longer the loud defiant howl, but a long, plaintive wail." Still the effort to catch Lobo went on, and he was lured to the ranch house where Blanca's body had been taken.

Soon, Lobo was found standing, traps clenched on all four legs. Seton raised his Winchester to finish the job. But, respecting the wolf's loyalty to his mate and dignified defiance, Seton could not bring himself to pull the trigger. Lobo was instead captured and taken to the ranch. Muzzled and chained, the big wolf ignored his human captors. Lobo died that night, as Seton thought, of a broken heart.

The events changed Seton. "Ever since Lobo, my sincerest wish has been to impress upon people that each of our native wild creatures is in itself a precious heritage that we have no right to destroy or put beyond the reach of our children," he wrote.

"The King of the Currumpaw, a Wolf Story" was first published in *Scribner's Magazine* in June 1894. As *Lobo, the King of Currumpaw*, it was the first

short story in Seton's enormously popular 1898 book *Wild Animals I Have Known*. The touching story is credited with changing the views on man's interaction with wild animals, then with launching the conservation movement. The title of a 2008 British documentary, *Lobo: The Wolf that Changed America*, illustrates the impact of Seton's Lobo story.

Seton would be a champion of wolves the rest of his life; thus, it is fitting that his Lobo story is shared with tens of thousands of visitors each year just miles removed from Currumpah Valley, where Lobo and his pack roamed.

A REAL RANCH

Through the decades, operations have maintained high Phillips standards

Philmont Scout Ranch is economically and perfectly named. "Philmont," with its nod to Waite Phillips and the majestic mountains; "Scout," a young-

Philmont wranglers drive a herd in the high country.

A lone buffalo grazes in the north country.

Opposite page: Buffalo have roamed their pastures at Philmont since the days of Waite Phillips.

ster whose life can be enriched at this place; and "Ranch," that romantic but rugged and icon of the American West.

When the Boy Scouts of America took deed of Philmont, it was quite some out-of-the-box thinking that the service organization would take over an impressive ranch operation. But Waite Phillips fully envisioned that visiting youth would see and participate in an operating cattle ranch.

Waite Phillips would certainly be proud that Philmont in 2008 received one of two awards for excellence by the New Mexico Society for Range Management. Not that 2008 was any different from any of the other years in which the Boy Scouts have operated the Philmont ranch, adhering throughout to the high Phillips standards.

Philmont generally maintains about 300 head of cattle, one hundred or so buffalo, a remuda of some 275 horses, and 120 burros.

Highway 21, from Cimarron to Philmont headquarters, neatly bisects the core of the ranching operations. Three buffalo pastures lie just to the west of the highway, encompassing 4,200 acres and extending to Webster Reservoir. The pastures are contained with tall, six-wire barbed wire fences, as buffalo have a deceptively amazing ability to jump. Bison have roamed this acreage since the Waite Phillips era. Philmont serves up a buffalo barbecue every Tuesday during summers at the Training Center.

A handful of winter cow pastures flank the north side of the Tooth of Time Ridge, and three others ring the west and north sides of Webster Reservoir.

With 240 horses in its program, Philmont tack rooms are full of bridles, ropes, and saddles.

Together, they comprise nearly 4,700 acres. This winter range is situated below an elevation of 7,500 feet. In summer, cattle are taken to higher grazing ground, up to 10,000 feet.

East and south of headquarters are found a 600-acre pasture for horses and 700 acres for bulls. In addition to grazing, all livestock enjoy supplemental feed during harsh stretches of winter, or during times of drought.

Philmont farms, too. Thirty-six acres of cropland, known as the "Big House Alfalfa," exists south of the ranch headquarters and north of the Villa Philmonte. To the east of the Villa and Training Center lie two irrigated parcels, each about 120 acres and watered with a center-point sprinkler. Irrigation water comes from 1,000 acre-feet of rights in Eagle Nest, diverted when needed from the Cimarron River. Hay is cut twice a year.

Philmont's ranging operations have been led by some outstanding and long-tenured cowboy bosses, including one with that name. Lawrence "Boss" Sanchez worked for Waite Phillips, then for the Boy Scouts. He became head horse wrangler in 1954, and served until his retirement in 1983. Also in 1954, Bill Littrell took the farm and ranch superintendent job, which he held for the next two decades. Philmont ran a herd of 500 Hereford cattle in his early days. Bob Knox and Bob Ricklefs have been ranching bosses in the most recent decades.

Philmont has boasted two Cattlemen of the Year, awarded by the New Mexico Cattle Growers Association. Littrell was honored in 1975, and Ricklefs in 2011. A trio of Philmont neighbors

Cowgirl Rachel Skaggs works with other wranglers to push about 200 head of cattle from Lover's Leap to Bonito Canyon in 2012. (Photo by Erin Nash, Philnews)

earned the award, as well: Les Davis of the CS Ranch in 1975, his wife Linda Davis in 1990, and Gretchen Sammis of the Chase Ranch in 2006.

GOOD NEIGHBORS

Philmont experiences extend onto nearby public, private tracts

The Philmont experience doesn't stop at Philmont boundaries. For fifty years, trekking Scouts have been privileged to hike and camp on about 86,000 acres of neighboring properties to the north and east, both public and private.

The largest tract consists of some 45,000 acres in the spectacular Valle Vidal wilderness section of

the Carson National Forest, bordering Philmont proper near the Dan Beard and Rich Cabins camps and the north Ponil country. Since 1988, Philmont's special use agreement with the U.S. Forest Service has required visiting Scouts to perform meaningful conservation service and practice Leave No Trace camping.

Some of Philmont's most popular programs, such as search and rescue, mountain biking, astronomy, and weather forecasting, are found on Valle Vidal itineraries. Few established trails are found in the wilderness, and some crews enjoy a "bushwhack" experience of navigating from location to location using only map and compass or GPS. Valle Vidal, 100,000 acres in all, was formerly part of the Vermejo Park ranch and donated by then-owner Pennzoil Corporation to the U.S.

After the Valle Vidal became public land, Philmont Scouts were allowed to hike across its scenic parks.

government in 1982. It's home to New Mexico's largest elk herd.

Philmont uses two sectors of Vermejo Park, also known as the WS Ranch, and today owned by cable magnate Ted Turner. One, the Greenwood Tract, serves as a corridor between Philmont and the Valle Vidal. It lies north of the Baldy Mountain area. The second WS parcel, the Heck Tract, sits on Philmont's eastern flank, just northeast of Cimarron. Since 2011, it has been utilized for starting and ending camps and offers a geocaching program. Both Vermejo Park tracts used by Philmont are roughly 12,000 acres in size.

Another Ponil-area neighbor ranch, the Kimberlin Ponil, grants backpackers access to the east end of the Valle Vidal through North Ponil Creek and Abran Canyon. No camping takes place.

Philmont participants also are allowed to hike across the Barker Wildlife Area, 5,400 acres straddling North Ponil Creek, just east of Vermejo's Greenwood piece. Philmont has had a Barker access agreement with the New Mexico Department of Game and Fish since 1964.

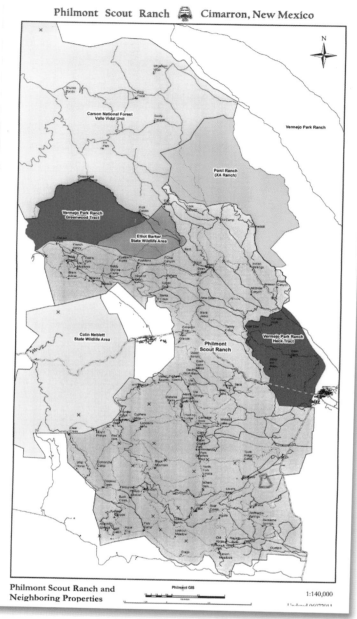
Philmont benefits with access to a handful of neighboring tracts.

To maintain neighbor partnerships, Philmont stresses to staff and visiting Scouts the importance of responsible use of the land. The ranch has obviously succeeded in that goal, with Exhibit A being the 2013 agreement to manage and use the neighboring Chase Ranch for the foreseeable future.

SECOND SEASON

After busy summer, plenty of activity can be seen

Prime time at Philmont consists of a twelve-week summer window from mid-June until late August, when the tens of thousands of Scouts and leaders take to the hills. To handle the onslaught, Philmont's seasonal employment soars into four digits.

At summer's end, activity slows, the summer staffers go back home to work or college, and the ranch gets back down to its eighty full-time employees.

But there remains a host of programs and a lot of activity in the following three seasons.

In September and October, Philmont offers Autumn Adventure expeditions. They have a variety of purposes, one simply being to hike the ranch in perfect fall weather and to enjoy the vibrant change of colors of the aspen trees and scrub oak. Some say fall, with warm days and cool nights, and with less trail traffic, is the best time on the ranch.

Other Autumn Adventure activities focus on letting adult and youth leaders get a taste of Philmont, so as to plan for a future trek for their group. All-adult

Winter adventurers travel by snowshoe to the backcountry.

Changing colors and a dash of snow enhance Baldy Mountain.

Opposite page: The Tooth of Time wears its own type of toothpaste.

crews, say from a given Boy Scout district or council, are allowed in the fall, unlike summer. An additional program centers on training to become an Advanced Educator in Leave No Trace camping methods.

When the weather gets really cold, participants in Philmont's Winter Adventure programs learn how to camp and stay "comfortably cool" in the elements. The expeditions are much shorter than summer treks, typically three days scheduled around weekends from late December to March, and staff guides accompany the crews for the duration. Activities include ski touring, avalanche safety, snow-shelter building, and winter ecology.

Elsewhere on the Scout Ranch, the Ranching Department has brought cattle down from higher summer pastures. Philmont administrators, one might think, might enjoy a slower pace during the cold months. Not the case. It takes months of plan-

ning and management to get ready for the coming summer, and projects put off during Philmont's prime time can finally get the full off-season attention they require.

Winter participants pick a path.

CHAPTER 6
PHILMONT TOMORROW

CHASE RANCH

On its seventy-fifth, Philmont gains long lease on historic ranch tract

On its seventy-fifth anniversary, Philmont Scout Ranch received a huge gift. Effective November 1, 2013, Philmont entered into a long-term lease to operate and preserve the historic Chase Ranch, its longtime neighbor in the Ponil country.

Philmont will maintain the 11,000-acre tract as a working ranch, and convert the historic ranch house into a museum that showcases the rich history of the Chase family and its western cattle-ranching way of life.

The agreement, made between Philmont and the Chase Ranch Foundation, fulfills the last wishes of the late owner of the ranch, legendary cattlewoman Gretchen Sammis. She was a great-granddaughter of Manly and Theresa Chase, who homesteaded the ranch in 1867. They had crossed Raton Pass in a wagon loaded with their all their worldly goods and bought a piece of the Maxwell Land Grant. The Chase Ranch remained continuously owned and operated by Chase descendants until Sammis passed away in August 2012.

"Long before she died, Gretchen mapped the future for Chase Ranch and facilitated this lasting legacy," said Thelma Coker of Cimarron, one of the founda-

tion's directors. "Gretchen was a fourth-generation rancher, a teacher and educator, a conservator, a lover of young people and of the land, a community member who delighted in sharing Chase Ranch with others and helping them appreciate its history, beauty, and generational worth. She wanted Chase Ranch to continue for generations as a historic model cattle ranch, and she wanted her family's history to be preserved."

Sammis served on the policy-setting Philmont Ranch Committee for many years. "Working with the Chase Ranch Foundation to help promote her wishes and dreams is one of the greatest things that has been asked of Philmont Scout Ranch," said John Clark, Philmont's general manager. "Gretchen has given guidance and support for our Ranch and Conservation Task Force. Together we have made the dreams of thousands of participants come true. Now we have an opportunity to make her dreams come true."

Those dreams have actually been in the Chase family for almost a century, as it turns out. Coincidentally, Philmont Museum staffers in 2013 discovered a previously unknown brochure for the "Kit Carson Camp," operated on the Chase Ranch by Mason and Stanley Chase, sons of ranch founders Manly and Theresa. The brochure was printed around 1923; it invites guests to come to the camp for "a real ranch vacation."

The Chase Ranch lies north of Cimarron.

Gretchen Sammis was a great-granddaughter of Manly and Theresa Chase.

"The aim of the camp is to provide a happy and interesting summer place for those who want to see the west," the brochure stated. "Here they will be met by guides with gentle saddle horses and taken to one of our mountain camps where they can fish and hunt and explore the mountain trails in all directions through beautifully timbered country, watered by crystal streams, and where they can thoroughly enjoy the outdoor life."

That description mirrored the vision of Waite Phillips, that his Philmont Ranch would become a "university of the out-of-doors" for young men.

The addition of the Chase Ranch acreage as part of Philmont—ranch officials stress that it is a long-

Mason Chase, far right, and his cow outfit paused for a photograph in the 1920s.

The early Chases understood that the Western ranching experience would have appeal to visitors.

The historic Chase Ranch house is set to become a museum to preserve the Chase story and highlight the cattle-ranching way of life.

term lease, and not an outright gift—came on the fiftieth anniversary of the Clapp donation, the last time the ranch saw formal border expansion, and by roughly the same acreage.

HIKE ON!

Philmont poised to continue tradition of innovative outdoor facility

Seventy-five years and a million Scouts. It's been a great, history-making ride at Philmont Scout Ranch. So far. While it's fun and enriching to look back at the past, those given the privilege of carrying out the vision and legacy of Waite Phillips have to be at all times moving forward, planning for the future.

The manner in which Philmont has progressed and been developed over these three-quarters of a century provides strong and comforting evidence

A crew hikes into the Whiteman Vega camp on the Valle Vidal.

The high country around Baldy Mountain.

that the ranch will continue to innovate and work to meet changing times.

Mark Anderson, Philmont's director of program, says this: "Going forward, we have to look at how we can better the resource. As the one-millionth Scout comes through in 2014, we need to be asking ourselves how will this special place look for the two-millionth Scout. Are we doing what we need to be doing?"

Philmont's mission statement remains to:

■ *Support the mission of the Boy Scouts of America.*

■ *Provide safe, challenging outdoor experiences for youth and adults, maximizing their physical, mental, and spiritual development.*

■ *Provide conferences and training for volunteer and professional Scouters.*

■ *Operate on a sound financial basis and to conserve and preserve resources.*

■ *Annually inspect the facility to ensure safety and program standards are being met.*

Philmont strives to share its opportunities with as many campers and leaders as possible. But even as early as in Philmont's second full decade, managers of the Scout Ranch knew that limitless attendance was not possible, that thoughtful utilization of the ranch's unparalleled but finite resources would be mandatory. That mindset continues today.

"I want Philmont to be a world-class facility, either leading in 'best practices' of how we manage our natural resources, or following those who are leading," says Anderson.

It is not just the managers who focus on the wise use of the land. In the new twenty-first century, Philmont began a concentrated emphasis on teaching its visiting Scouts and leaders the principles of Leave No Trace outdoor ethics. Leave No Trace, implemented in partnership with outdoor equipment maker JanSport, has seven core principles: plan and prepare, travel and camp on durable surfaces, dispose of waste properly, leave what you find, minimize campfires, respect wildlife, and be considerate of others. Leave No Trace, together with the

Philmont allows cell phones in the backcountry (though many areas don't have coverage), but encourages Scouts to break free from their screens.

Philmont strives for excellence in its conservation works, and trail building is carefully planned.

The Philmont experience lifts spirits and instills confidence in young Scouters.

Philmont Wilderness Pledge program and BEEP, the Backcountry Environmental Education Program, bodes well for Philmont's physical future. Philmont is also a member of the Sustainable Forestry Initiative.

With a flurry of ambitious new initiatives in 2013, it seemed as if Philmont's seventy-fifth year was fortuitous, perhaps the advent of a new era.

Without a doubt, the biggest development was the Chase Ranch agreement, expanding Philmont's managed boundaries for the first time in fifty years. A $6-million expansion of the Philmont Museum and Seton Memorial Library was initiated. And plans were being set to highlight two forms of early transportation in the Cimarron country, first with the reconstruction of two miles of railroad track in the Ponil country and a themed camp, then with major development efforts at Rayado through the year 2021, the bicentennial of the Santa Fe Trail. Lastly and importantly, in 2013, the Philmont Staff Association launched an ambitious Campaign4Philmont to raise $1.4 million for four projects: replacing the advisors' meeting facility at Camping Headquarters, furnishing the backcountry camps, facility improvements at the Philmont Training Center, and scholarship support for seasonal staff.

Yes, the Philmont future shines as brightly as it ever has.

At seventy-five, Philmont Scout Ranch continues to carry out the mission first envisioned in 1938, and to fully satisfy the aspirations as described on a plaque mounted on a wall of the gazebo in what once was Waite and Genevieve Phillips' summer home.

These properties
Are donated and dedicated
To the Boy Scouts of America
For the purpose of perpetuating
Faith—Self-Reliance—Integrity—Freedom
Principles used to build this great country by
The American Pioneer

So that
These future citizens may
Through thoughtful adult guidance
And by the inspiration of nature
Visualize and for a code of living
To diligently maintain these high ideals
And our proper destiny

Waite Phillips
December 31, 1941

Sunrise at Baldy Mountain.

BIBLIOGRAPHY AND FURTHER READING

Bates, Dave and Susan. *The Philmont Field Guide.* Media Studio, Boy Scouts of America, 2012.

Carter, David E. *Philmont, A Timeless Experience.* London Books Ltd., 2002.

Cass, William F. *The Last Flight of Liberator 41-1133.* William F. Cass, 1996.

Huffman, Minor S. *High Adventure Among the Magic Mountains, Philmont the First 50 Years.* TIBS, Inc., 1988.

Murphy, Lawrence R. *Philmont, A History of New Mexico's Cimarron Country.* University of New Mexico Press, 1987.

Poppenhouse, Jerry. *Philmont, Where Spirits Soar.* Rodgers Lithographing Co., 1989.

Rohrbacher, Rock. *Philmanac, A Trekker's Guide to the Philmont Backcountry.* CSS Publishing, 2012.

Wallis, Michael. *Beyond the Hills, The Journey of Waite Phillips.* Oklahoma Heritage Association, 2005.

Wertz, William C. *Phillips, The First 66 Years.* Phillips Petroleum Company, 1983.

Zimmer, Stephen and Larry Walker. *Philmont, A Brief History of the New Mexico Scout Ranch.* Sunstone Press, 2000.

Zimmer, Stephen and Larry Walker. *Philmont, An Illustrated History.* Smith & Associates, 1988.

Zimmer, Stephen and Nancy Klein. *Vision, Grace and Generosity, The Story of Waite and Genevieve Phillips and the Philmont Scout Ranch.* Lufkin Printing Company, 2002.